What A Difference
A Line Can Make

Larry L. Booker

**LIGHTHOUSE
PUBLICATIONS**

What A Difference A Line Can Make
by Larry Booker

Published in the United States of America.
Printed in the United States of America.

Library of Congress Control Number: 2002103416

ISBN 0-9717329-0-6
U.S. $10.95 / CAN $15.95

Cover illustration by Mary Yoder
Design by Matt Jones & Jason Lamb of 7Dcreative.com

For publications and tapes please contact:

Lighthouse Publications
PO Box 520
Rialto, CA 92377
Phone: 909-820-2393
Fax: 909-820-2323
www.inlandlighthouse.com

To the best friend I ever had;
my Saviour to whom I owe everything.

Table Of Contents

Legend

Note: All Scripture references are from the King James Version unless otherwise noted. Occasionally (KJV) *is* noted to make sure of clarification. In all scriptures given, any highlighting done in **'bold print'** has obviously been done by the author. When other translations are used, their abbreviations are shown and are as follows:

American Standard Version ....ASV
New American Standard Bible...................................NASB
Berkely..Ber
Conybeare ....Con
Goodspeed.. Gspd
Ronald Knox ....Knox
George Lamsa .... Lam
James Moffet...Mof
Helen Montgomery .... Mon
New English Bible ....NEB
Olaf Norlie .... NOR
J.B. Phillips .... Phi
C.H. Rieu ....Rieu
J.B. Rotherham...Rhm
Kenneth Taylor..Tay
John Wycliffe .... Wyc
New International Version .... NIV
New American Standard Bible...................................NASB

Acknowledgements

Space does not allow, nor can mere words express my appreciation to the host of people that have inspired, enlightened, encouraged, and helped me with this book. First and foremost I must thank my immediate family—my wife and three sons—for making this treatise concerning sanctity towards our Lord much easier than it could have otherwise been. The fact that they have ever stood with me in my stands and teachings have made my ministry 'a piece of cake' compared to the struggles I've known others to face. Brenda, Joel, Phillip and Larry Andy, I thank you from my heart for your heartfelt support through the years and for your encouragement in the project of this book. I also want to say 'Thank You' to Phillip Wayne and Larry Andrew for your patience and help with an 'old fossil' that knows next to nothing about computers. Without your expertise (literally), what has taken two years (off and on) would probably never been finished. If nothing else, sheer exasperation would have 'done me in.'

I wish to extend my appreciation to the man that God greatly used to make 'a little something' out of that which was "without form and void," my pastor, Roy Moss of Bartlesville, Oklahoma. Brother Moss, I thank you for instilling into the heart of a nineteen year old 'hippie' the truths of God and His holiness.

Were he still here with us, I would like to thank Rev. David Gray for his oft encouragement for me to "Take up the pen" and write. As Rev. J.R. Ensey *is* still with us I would like to thank him for doing the same. I also want to thank Bro. Ensey's 'helper of many years,' Paul Sibley, for his words of support, as well as his help in editing. I also thank Paul, Adam Pierce and my son Joel for taking up so much of the daily 'slack' around the church, in order to free up some of my time that I could spend it on this project. I must also thank Rev. Ralph McGuire of Marion, Wisconsin, for his literally years of encouragement for me to write as well as his many fine suggestions and instructions on how a writer must "find his style."

Special thanks to Sister Beth Baus for transcribing nine of these chapters from taped messages that I had taught in our church—after which I set about to forge into 'coherent shape.' It was a mammoth undertaking on her part. I also want to thank her for keeping track of the paper trail and mess that I tend to leave behind, as well as the handling of all things mailed in this project as well as many others. Again, it is no small feat and I appreciate it.

Sister Michelle DeGood of Fresno was very instrumental in editing as well as in patiently sending me her finished work—over and over again. If she ever grew frustrated, she never showed it. Michelle's pastor and my friend of many years, Rev. Vaughn Morton, has been a Godsend to me in more ways than I can number. Vaughn—you are a true friend and I value your encouragement in this as well as in many of our other 'projects.'

My thanks to Sister Mary Yoder for her artistry that became the cover for this book and her dedication to the Kingdom of God and all its endeavors. You are a blessing.

May God richly bless Pastor Gerry Marin for his translation of this work into the beautiful Spanish language. It was a tremendous undertaking and I am ever in his debt. Thank you Brother Marin, you are a great man and a great blessing.

To my friend, Nathaniel Wilson for the 'Forward' as well as some very cogent insights and into various portions of the text of this book.

To Rev. and Mrs. Wayne Chennault (Mom & Dad) I say "Thank You" for thirty years of prayer *for* me and faith *in* me. I could not have made it without you.

And I must here express my heartfelt appreciation, yea more than appreciation, for the hundreds of ministers that God has brought across the path of my life. It is due to the thousands of hours of preaching, teaching, counsel and friendship that I have been the recipient of that I am able to write this book. While I'd like to think that a large part of this is my inspiration—I know better. Probably only eternity will reveal that this book is merely a compilation of things I have been taught, heard preached or discussed around countless auditoriums, tables and dens through the years. After all, this is also God's plan and way of doing business.

"Iron sharpens iron, so one man sharpens another." (Proverbs 27:17, New American Standard)

"For none of us liveth to himself, and no man dieth to himself." (Rom 14:7)

Finally—and most important of all—I sincerely want to express my eternal love and gratefulness to my Lord and Savior Jesus Christ. Without His mercy, love and patience with me through the years, this book as well as everything else good in my life would have been utterly impossible. My first nineteen years more than adequately proved that—but more about that… later.

My earnest prayer therefore is that this work may be a help to others, who desire to please God and know more of Him.

Forward

In the late 1960's, during the Vietnam conflict, a picture was in the newspaper of a young college-age man. To show opposition to the war and the military draft he was holding a sign which declared: "Nothing is worth dying for." Seeing the sign, someone made the observation that if nothing is worth dying for, then does anything remain worth living for?

It is a good question. Lacking anything which has ultimate value, life, in turn, loses its own value. Proceeding from this is an ongoing diminution of everything that has to do with life. Nothing matters. Appetites rule. The end result is meaninglessness and absurdity.

In contrast to this is life in Christ. In Him, life goes the other direction. Rather than dumbing life down, He vivifies it-makes it more abundant, more important. Man is made in God's image. No longer viewed as just "glorified dirt," a whole new panorama of meaning is attached to one's life, purpose, conduct, and actions. Former drifters with no mission or meaning are now God-bearers, temples, sanctuaries, revealers of the hidden, the divine, the other-worldly. They have transcended finitude, tasted the infinite, been commissioned with a ministry of reconciliation and become a part of a universal cause. Everything is now important, has meaning, and comes bearing a message. This is the thinking behind this book. You are important and everything you do is important.

I gently suggest you read carefully and charitably the contents. Ponder deeply and reflect long about whether extended time and space would have been used in scripture to discuss things that we, in this later day, would later be expected by God to discard as simply being cultural and time-dated for people long ago. Casually and cavalierly tossing aside scriptural subjects which seem to cross present cultural mores and standards (or the lack of them), without considering whether or not they contain meaning and purpose beyond some ancient circumstance, is being done by people that seemingly ought to know better. Larry Booker provides a refreshing contrast to this and, moving against the grain of modern evangelical thought, approaches his subject with the uncanny postmodern insight that, perhaps more than any other time since the early church, our time is eerily like that one—a time in which these kinds of truths are experiencing an authentic revival of relevance.

Dr. Nathaniel J. Wilson

Preface

God had a church in mind before there was ever height, depth, length, breadth, a universe, or even one angel to applaud the creation of all such. That church is the one I wish to pastor, and it should be the desire of every pastor for his congregation to be the church God had in mind "from before the foundation of the earth." That doesn't mean that we attain 'perfection' here, or that there won't be problems. Even though it is His church, it does contain faults, foibles, frailties, it will have errors and will make mistakes. That is the reason God has instituted an 'altar' that we can "...come boldly unto the throne of grace to obtain mercy and find grace to help in time of need." (Hebrews 4:16) If the ministry becomes focused only on the church's deficiencies, it will lead only to more difficulty and endless frustration. Our focus must remain on God, His grace, His glory, His power, and God's desire for the lost to be saved.

It is also God's will that His children, "...all come in the unity of the faith, and of the knowledge of the Son of God, unto a perfect man, unto the measure of the stature of the fulness of Christ." (Eph 4:13)

To accomplish this we must give our time and attention to all of the teachings of the word of God. This book is therefore dedicated to those truths that God especially honors when found in His people: Righteousness, Godliness, Holiness and Truth. I have written this book in hope that it might be of help to men and women who desire to honor God and His church, and that God might recognize it as being what He had in mind; "According as he hath chosen us in him before the foundation of the world, that we should be holy and without blame before him in love." (Eph 1:4)

Chapter One

When God Overthrows

We begin this book purposely with the subject 'When God Overthrows.' Though He would much rather *keep and bless*—whether we like it—or believe it—God on occasion does overthrow that with which He is not pleased. When He does, we want to be part of the number that He keeps and blesses. Throughout scripture we see that while; "…His anger endureth but a moment; in his favour is life…" (Ps 30:5)

Nowhere is this seen with more clarity than in the book of Numbers.

***

The book of Numbers is about Israel, the church in the wilderness. Israel was a people, 70 souls in number, when they entered the land of Egypt at the bidding of Joseph and the providence of God. They were there for 430 years, and during that time they grew exceedingly in *number* (hence the name of the book). By the time they left Egypt they had a standing army of men 600,000 strong. This did not include the aged men, nor the men who were under 20. If we give each of these numbered men a wife and only 2 children it comes to 2-1/2 million people, minimum. Seventy souls had grown to somewhere in the neighborhood of 3 million people.

We are told in I Corinthians 10 that these are our fathers. "**Moreover, brethren, I would not that ye should be ignorant, how that all our fathers were under the cloud and all passed through the sea; And were all baptized unto Moses in the cloud and in the sea;**

And did all eat the same spiritual meat; And did all drink the same spiritual drink: for they drank of that spiritual Rock that followed them: and that Rock was Christ. **But with many of them God was not well pleased: for they were overthrown in the wilderness.** Now these things were our examples, to the intent that we should not lust after evil things, as they also lusted. Neither be ye idolaters, as were some of them; as it is written, The people sat down to eat and drink, and rose up to play. Neither let us commit fornication, as some of them committed, and fell in one day three and twenty thousand. Neither let us tempt Christ, as some of them also tempted, and were destroyed of serpents. Neither murmur ye, as some of them also murmured, and were destroyed of the destroyer. Now all these things happened unto them for ensamples: and they are written for our admonition, upon whom the ends of the world are come. Wherefore let him that thinketh he standeth, take heed lest he fall." (I Corinthians 10:1-12)

While we are not—for the most part—Hebrews after the flesh, we are sons of Abraham after the faith. Paul therefore is speaking spiritually when he writes to us Gentiles that, "Brethren, I would not that ye should be ignorant, how that all our fathers were under the cloud, and all passed through the sea; And were all baptized unto Moses in the cloud and in the sea."

When "our fathers" left Egypt by way of great deliverance and a Red Sea crossing, they became the Church on the move. We of this dispensation have come to the church—to the household of faith—the heavenly Jerusalem—the city of the living God—by obedience to the gospel. We found the foreordained place of death, burial and resurrection. We die in repentance, are buried with Him in baptism and rise to walk in newness of life through the gift of the Holy Ghost (read Romans 6:4). To enter the church of the living God, we are now baptized in water in the name of Jesus Christ and in His Spirit. (see John 3:5 & Acts 2:38) Our fathers were baptized in water in the Red Sea unto Moses, and they were baptized in Spirit by the glory cloud. They all did eat the same spiritual meat when they ate the heavenly manna. They all drank the same spiritual drink when they drank from that rock which followed them; that rock, Paul states, was Christ. But though they (and we) had all of these things in common, the Bible says, "But with many of them God was not well pleased."

***

I lean on your familiarity with the errors of the Israelites. Some of them did not even get past the Red Sea before they accused Moses of bringing them out to be slain. "...because there were no graves in Egypt, hast thou taken us away to die in the wilderness? Wherefore hast thou dealt thus with us...?" (Exodus 14:11) Three days later, even after they witnessed the drowning of Pharoah's army as well as the 10 plagues of Egypt, they murmured against Moses because they had come to a place of bitter waters. God heard this and was not well pleased. You would think the Israelites would realize that a God who could produce 10 great plagues, as well as destroy Pharoah's army in the Red Sea, could take care of His people in the wilderness—but how soon they forgot. Upon instruction from God, Moses cut down a tree and cast it into the waters. The waters were healed and the people drank. This was but the first of many temptations in the wilderness whereby the people of God—for the most part—failed Him, in spite of the victories He had wrought for them.

They finally came to Kadesh Barnea, a place that was just a few steps, if you please, from the 'promise land.' They had been in the wilderness for one year and it was time to go up and possess the country. However, the people asked Moses, 'Before we go up, why don't we send out princes of the tribes and let them spy out the country?' Moses—and more importantly—God, agreed.

The 12 men went out, spied out the land and returned in 40 days. They all agreed that, 'It is a land that is good, and it indeed flows with milk and honey. It is everything we were told it would be.' But 10 of them went on to give an evil report, 'There are giants there. There are walled cities there. We are like grasshoppers in the sight of the sons of Anak, and we are not able to do this.' This unbelief and fear became the proverbial straw that broke the camels back with God. He said, 'That's it, you're not going up. I refuse to let this generation go up. I will eventually allow those aged 20 and under to go, and I will allow the 2 faithful spies Joshua and Caleb to go. No one else is going.'

God's judgment was that Israel spend a year of wandering for each day they had spied out the land of promise. Forty years they wandered in the wilderness of Sinai before He took a new generation up into the land of Canaan. We must picture clearly in our minds and our hearts that everybody 20 years and older died having never entered the land of promise. An entire generation fell short of the promise of God.

It is also important that we understand that during this time there was ongoing birth and growth as families continued to beget children and grandchildren during those 40 years.

The Numbering of the People

In the beginning of the book of Numbers the people were numbered, that is, the men of fighting age. Each tribe was counted except the tribe of Levi. Levi was a separate entity, the priesthood to the nation.[1] The two sons of Joseph, Ephraim and Manasseh, were each considered a tribe and these made up 12 tribes.

They were numbered as follows:

Reuben	-	46,500;
Simeon	-	59,300;
Gad	-	49,650;
Judah	-	74,600;
Issachar	-	54,400;
Zebulun	-	57,700;
Ephraim	-	40,500;
Manasseh	-	42,200;

Benjamin	-	35,400;
Dan	-	62,700;
Asher	-	41,500;
Naphtali	-	53,400.

This gave Israel a standing army of 603,550 men, of which God said none but Joshua and Caleb would enter the promised land.

Thus this church in the wilderness began her sojourn. While sons and daughters were continually being born into the congregation, others in the congregation were continually dying. The people wandered in this state of affairs for 40 years, until God had cleared the slate of all who were over 20 years of age at the time of the provocation.

It would be spiritually healthy for us today to realize that though we are in the dispensation of grace—and we understand "His great love wherewith He loved us" (Eph. 2:4)—we cannot forget that Jesus Christ is "the same yesterday, today and forever" (Hebrews 13:8). God is a God of love but He is also a God of holiness as well as being a God of judgment. There are far more Biblical references to the holiness of God than to the love of God. That does not negate His love, but rather is meant to shed light into our hearts and minds that His love is first of all—*very holy in its nature*. As a holy God, He wants and expects a holy people.

In the wilderness they all drank the same spiritual drink and all ate the same spiritual meat. They were all baptized in the sea and in the cloud, *"but with many of them God was not well pleased."* The Word of God takes ample time to inform us of the various sins of the people and the ensuing judgments of God that took place in the wilderness.

In Chapter 11 a plague struck Israel while the much lusted-after quail was still in their teeth.

In Chapter 16 Korah, Dathan and Abiram, the sons of Levi, rose up in rebellion against Moses and Aaron, only to be swallowed up alive by the earth and sent straight down to the pit. This judgment was quickly followed by a plague upon the chiding, rebellious congregation who blamed Moses for the deaths of the rebels. In Chapter 21 we read of a further plague of fiery serpents that was sent among the people because of their murmuring against Moses and Aaron. Chapter 25 tells of yet another plague because the people joined with Moab at Baalpeor in eating meat sacrificed to the Moabite gods, and sinned yet further by fornicating with the Moabite women.

By the time you get to the end of the book of Numbers, it is over for that generation. When the last hoary head died, and the 40-year judgment had lapsed, God finally said, 'It is time…go up and possess the country.'

The Second Numbering

Just before they went into the land of Canaan God commanded to number the people again.

Reuben now has	-	43,730;
Simeon	-	22,200;
Gad	-	40,500;
Judah	-	76,500;
Issachar	-	64,300;
Zebulun	-	60,500;
Ephraim	-	32,500;
Manasseh	-	52,700;
Benjamin	-	46,500;
Dan	-	64,400;
Asher	-	53,400;
Naphtali	-	45,400.

A total of 601,730 men of fighting age.

Thus He gives us the final tally so that we know the beginning *and* the end. In this last numbering Israel has lost 1,820 people. They've gone in the red. That may not seem like much of a decrease, but when one considers the following facts it is in actuality, appalling.

If the 70 people who came to Goshen grew to a number of at least 2-1/2 million in 400 years, then 2-1/2 million people in another 40 years should have grown tremendously. One might say; "But it was only 40 years." Forty years is one-tenth the time of 400 years—they should have grown at least one-tenth. Instead of being 1,820 less, they should have been 200,000 more. They had nutritious food provided every day. Their clothes did not wear out. They had all the water they needed. They should have proliferated. But in the wilderness they did not grow—they decreased.

However, that 1,820 diminishing does not tell the whole story, nor does the simple fact that they were sinful and plagued in the wilderness. While some of the tribes decreased, some tribes *actually grew*, and quite astoundingly at that, especially considering all the sins and judgments. Note the large increase of 20,500 in the tribe of Manasseh, and 10,200 in Benjamin.

As we read the final number of these tribes, the ending balances compared to the beginning tell an important tale. Reuben lost 2,770; Gad lost 5,150; Judah gained 1,900. Issachar, of whom it was said in David's day "had an understanding of times and knew what Israel ought to do," gained 9,900. Zebulun gained 2,800. Ephraim lost 8,000, while Manasseh his brother gained 20,500. Benjamin gained 10,200; Dan gained 1,700; Asher gained 11,900; Naphtali lost 8,000.

But when it comes to the total profit and loss, it is breathtaking to realize that 60% of all the losses incurred was—by one tribe—Simeon's. Reuben received a 'slap' from God by losing 2,770. Ephraim received a 'blow' by losing 8,000, and Naphtali the same. But when God came to Simeon, it was as if He rolled up His sleeve, drew back His fist and 'floored them.' **This one tribe lost 37,100 men.**

Simeon

Where did Simeon go wrong? What did this tribe do to incur such wrath from God? Whatever it was, whatever mistakes they made, however they erred in their heart, God of Heaven please don't let me or this end-time church err in the same manner. Paul said that these things were written for our examples because we are the people upon whom the end of the world has come.

Although every one of the 12 tribes were Israelites, each individual tribe had distinct characteristics. This is seen just prior to Jacob's death in Egypt when he blessed his 12 sons. The prophecies he delivered reveal differences that were already emerging in them, and that would be carried over to their descendants.

In a similar manner Moses, before God took him away by death, gave prophetic blessings and prophecies to the tribes, noting their distinct differences and characteristics (Exodus 49). These tribes together made up the church in the wilderness—"but with all of them God was not well pleased."

I am not going to enumerate all of the differences between the tribes that scripture reveals. I will however concentrate on just a few of the tribes, their prophecies and fulfillment.

Concerning the tribe of Dan, the Spirit could see things that did not bode well for the future. "Dan shall be a serpent by the way, an adder in the path that biteth the horse heels so that his rider shall fall backward. (Genesis 49:17) It is believed that, in addition to being the most idolatrous people in the history of Israel, the tribe of Dan never repented of their idolatry. When the golden calves were set up in Dan and Beersheba by King Jeroboam, the nation eventually found a place of repentance and purging, but Dan never did (hence their being omitted from Revelation chapter 7). It is also believed by many that Judas Iscariot—the only one of the disciples who was not of the area of Galilee—was of the tribe of Dan and thus fulfilled the role of the biting serpent. Again, thousands of years before,

Jacob could see the trend and he spoke of it.

Concerning Simeon and Levi, God spoke through Jacob and said, "Simeon and Levi are brethren, instruments of cruelty are in their habitations...for in their anger they slew a man and in their selfwill they digged down a wall. Cursed be their anger for it was fierce; and their wrath for it was cruel. I will divide them in Jacob, and scatter them in Israel." (Genesis 49:5-7) The backdrop for this prophecy is found in Genesis 34, when Jacob's only daughter Dinah had been defiled sexually by one of the neighboring Hivite people, a man named Shecham. He loved Dinah however and wanted to marry her and do her honor. Jacob's sons devised that Israel would never have affinity with the Hivites unless every man and male child was circumcised. Shecham, who was the king's son and a noble man, loved Dinah so much that he said, 'We will do it.' Thus all the male inhabitants of their domain were circumcised.

On the third day after their circumcision, when the men of that city could not even move for the pain, Simeon and Levi came into the town and slew every male. They killed men who were suffering greatly in their attempt to placate Jacob's house—men who could not defend themselves nor even rise to flee. Thus in Genesis 49, when it comes time for Jacob to bless his sons and speak of future things, the Spirit speaks of Simeon and Levi's self-will—anger—fierce wrath—and that instruments of cruelty were in their habitations. They were doomed to be a people scattered amongst the nation, having no certain dwelling place as did the other tribes. This prophecy was of course fulfilled.

Although both of these men performed a hard and bitter act, I personally believe that there was an element in Levi that was not in Simeon. In Levi there seems to be a genuine righteous indignation against what happened to his sister that does not seem to be present in Simeon. While this does not excuse Levi or make what he did right, he seems to have had the purer motive. I base this on later actions performed by Levi's descendants, such as when Moses descended Mount Sinai after fasting for 40 days and nights. He came down from the mount with the glory of God upon him—to the sound of music, dancing and playing. The children of Israel (at least a portion of them) were naked and dancing before a golden calf[2], saying, "...as for this man Moses, we wot not has become of him."

Moses appeal was, "Who is on the Lord's side? Let him come unto me. And all the sons of Levi gathered themselves together unto him. And he said unto them, Thus saith the Lord God of Israel, put every man his sword by his side, and go in and out from gate to gate throughout the camp, and slay every man his brother, and every man his companion, and every man his neighbor. And the Children of Levi did according to the word of Moses: and there fell that day of the people about three thousand men." (Exodus 32:26-28) Note Simeon's absence in this act of retribution. Where is his righteous indignation now?

Levi could be tough, even ruthless, but in the midst of his hardness was a strain that said, 'What is right is right, and what is wrong is wrong.' No doubt there was overkill—as in the instance with Dinah, Shecham and the Hivite people—but indignation was there, none-theless. We don't see this in Simeon. Simeon simply had a blood lust. We never see his descendants being standouts for righteous-ness—in fact, we see just the opposite.

There is a sparseness of clues regarding the judgment meted out to the tribe of Simeon. When you have few clues, the ones you do have are very important. The negatives that we know about Simeon are that he was a companion to Levi in the slaying of the Hivite men. We also know that he did not stand with Levi when the idolatry at Sinai was judged, though Jacob had referred to their companion-ship. Outside of that, we have no clues to this heavy judgment of God, except one, and that is in the book of Numbers.

***

Balaam the son of Beor, the infamous but effective prophet, was hired by Balak, king of Moab to curse Israel. After a fascinating tale of his conscience searing, the talking ass, and weak protestations of innocence and integrity by Balaam, we finally find him offering up 7 Moabite rams and 7 oxen (he actually had Balak's men do it) to God. He did this in hopes of somehow enchanting God into cursing Israel through him, so that he might receive Balak's financial reward. Balaam says to God, "I have prepared 7 altars, and I have offered upon every altar a bullock and a ram." (Numbers 23:4) Again, he wants to bribe God with offerings in order to get Him to curse Israel for his own selfish, greedy ends. As he looked out across the tribes set in their stations, the Lord put a word (prophecy) in his mouth:

"Balak the king of Moab brought me from Aram...saying, Come curse me Jacob, and come, defy Israel. How shall I curse whom God hath not cursed? Or how shall I defy whom the Lord hath not defied? For from the tops of the rocks I see him, and from the hills I behold him: Lo, people shall dwell alone, and shall not be reckoned among the nations. Who can count the dust of Jacob, and number the fourth part of Israel? Let me die the death of the righteous and let my last end be like his!" (verses 7-10)

Then the Spirit lifted. What Balaam had uttered in the Spirit—God meant. What Balaam said concerning his desire to die righteously—he meant, to the depths of his compromised, twisted and tormented soul. At that point Balak waxed angry and said, "What hast thou done unto me? I took you to curse mine enemies, and behold thou hast blessed them altogether." (23:11) Two more times, at different locations, Balaam has 7 rams and 7 bullocks offered up, but to no avail. He can't get a curse out of God... only blessings. Balaam had received some of the most powerful prophetic utterances found in the Bible. Too late, he realized that there was "no enchantment against Israel." (23:23)

Balak finally said; "Therefore now flee thou to thy place: I thought to promote thee unto great honour; but, lo, the LORD hath kept thee back from honour." (24:11)

Balaam left, but not before cursing the Moabites, Edomites, Amlekites and Kenites. He hurled curses everywhere and in every direction, venting his spleen while being under the anointing of God (a feat still accomplished by some today) then returned to his house.

But in short order, Balaam coldly, cunningly and chillingly came back. He returned with the error of his heart still intact. He didn't care about Moab, Edom or Amelek. He didn't care about Israel. He had a vendetta against God for making him look like a fool, and he wanted Balak's gold. And he now had a 'new doctrine' whereby God would indeed curse Israel.

Balaam told Balak, 'I now know how to get God to destroy Israel.' Balak was all ears. Balaam said, 'You've got to get God to overthrow them. I can't do it, but if you can get them to perform wickedness, to do things that are vile in the sight of God, it will provoke God and He will overthrow them.' Balak asked, 'Like what?' Balaam then began to spin his spell.

Israel, with all their tribes, had been eating manna in the wilderness for many years. They lusted for quail and on one occasion because of their lustful, unthankful nature, God sent a plague and slew thousands while the quail was still in their teeth. Balaam had a plan to get God to slay Israel by inciting the lusts of the people that were ever just below the surface of their being.

Off in the distance from the camp of Israel were the sons of Moab. The Moabites offered meat to their false gods and while they were offering it, a breeze blew the smell of this roasted meat into the nostrils of the meat-starved Israelites. Then the Moabites brought it to them and they ate until their bellies were full and sated. Meanwhile, in the distance they saw something else; Balak had scoured Moab and brought the low, the lewd, and the willing young women. Israel went beserk. Having already eaten the meat sacrificed to idols, their consciences were weakened and defiled. With their convictions already compromised, they easily fell into fornication.

Balaam couldn't get God to curse them, but their own sin provoked

God into it. As soon as Israel began to commit fornication with the Moabite women after eating the idol-ridden meat, the plague began. Then, while the godly leadership of Israel mourned in the tabernacle, a man came to the door of the tent. On his arm was his newly acquired Moabite girlfriend. He looked at these old 'fuddy-duddies' crying because of immorality, weeping because of the lewdness that was now literally plaguing Israel. He laughed. He thought it was funny—a good joke. He then took his girlfriend and went into his tent. His name was Zimri, and he was a prince of the tribe of—Simeon.

But at that point, a man stood up in the midst of the weeping congregation—of the tribe of Levi, named Phinehas. It had been a long time coming, but Simeon and Levi were about to have a parting of the ways. 'We used to be together, Simeon. We slew side by side in ages gone by. I still possess the zeal in my heart for righteousness, but Simeon, somehow you never understood. I did what I did for a different cause, for righteous reasons, out of zealous motives. I may not have always been right, but I always loved what was right.'

So, while others wept, wailed and sobbed, Phinehas went out from the Tabernacle, took a spear from his tent, and made his way towards the giggling, laughing, audacious, promiscuous Simeonite. Zimri thought life was a lark. He thought holiness, separation and godliness were things of a different age. To him, the sacred was something to be laughed at, mocked and made fun of. Zimri's motto was, 'I will do what I want to do.'

Phinehas had a completely different perspective on life and God. He took the spear and went into Zimri's tent. The laughter turned to screams as, with one fell swoop, he killed them both. Most important for our consideration is—the moment he slew the two brazen fornicators—the plague ceased.

In the tabernacle the cry was, 'What is this church in the wilderness coming to? What is going to happen to us? What is becoming of us?' But one man took a spear and in righteous indignation, in a few seconds time, stopped the plague in its tracks. What did God think of this act? "And the Lord spake unto Moses saying Phinehas, the son of Eleazar, the son of Aaron the priest, hath turned away my wrath from the children of Israel, while he was zealous for my sake among them, that I consumed not the children of Israel in my jealousy. Wherefore say, behold, **I give unto him my covenant of peace. And he shall have it, and his seed after him, even the covenant of an everlasting priesthood; because he was zealous for his God, and made atonement for the children of Israel.**" (Numbers 25:10-13) From that day forward, the priesthood was assured in Levi.

Tribes of Today

My observation has been that as Israel was, so the church is. I've been a pastor for over two decades and have been preaching for over three. I have witnessed a number of interesting things during this time. I have been to numerous churches, campmeetings and conferences. I have seen many things both in and outside various organizational circles and fellowships, and have come to realize that—just as Israel had its various tribes with their individual characteristics, so the church is made up of various 'tribes' with their own unique characteristics. This is true not only on national and international levels, but also on district, sectional and even local church levels. I am not saying that this is wrong—it is simply a fact of life.

The church has all types of people who are blessed in different areas. They have different gifts, callings and ministries. Yet we all drink of the same spiritual drink; we have the Holy Ghost and draw from the same fount. We have all been baptized in Jesus' name. We have the same Word of God, and can therefore receive the same spiritual meat, though it may be served in different forms, styles and seasonings. [The 'flavor' depends upon the 'chef,' that is, the Minister and his background and personality]

While we should all be people of prayer, there are some who God has seemingly graced to pray more than others; it is a ministry with them. While they also give to the work in other ways, prayer is the chief item they seem to have to offer. This is absolutely invaluable to any local church.

There are others who, though they pray, seem to have been raised up to bless the work in other ways as well. Some have leadership abilities, or organizational talents, while others are exceptionally able to bless with finance. (read Romans 12:3-8 and I Corinthians 4:7)

We all should witness profusely, but there are some saints to whom this seems to come more natural and easy than for others. There are 'tribes' of saints who are more given to study than others; they love to delve into the deep things of the Word of God. They will study to a degree that is just not for everyone. This doesn't mean if people do not enjoy study, or prayer, or giving, or witnessing to the same degree that they are lost, or inferior to one another. It simply means they differ one from the other. It is good to consider in this discussion the words of the Apostle Paul:

"For who maketh thee to differ from another? and what hast thou that thou didst not receive? now if thou didst receive it, why dost thou glory, as if thou hadst not received it?" (1 Corinthians 4:7)

"For who regards you as superior? What do you have that you did not receive? And if you did receive it, why do you boast as if you had not received it?" (NASU)

There are tribes of people with musical abilities and within those tribes are 'sub-tribes' with likes and dislikes concerning different styles of music. It comes with the territory. I happen to be one of those eclectic people who enjoy all styles of gospel music— except so-called 'gospel rock;' *that*, I cannot abide. One might say that I am biased. Personally, I don't think God likes it either—for a number of *very good* reasons—but again… that's my tribe.

We need to understand that although the twelve tribes of Israel intermarried and fellowshipped with one another, they nevertheless retained, in varying degrees, their own special uniqueness and individuality. This is displayed for our instruction and understanding, and to help give us guidance in these last days. The tribe of Manasseh was not hell-bound and the tribe of Judah Heaven-bound because of their distinct characteristics. It was not a case of 'Ephraim, kiss it good-bye because you don't think like Benjamin.' Issachar was not 'out of it' because he didn't have the same feel for the sea and ships that Asher had.

People who allow deep divisions over *preferences* are simply carnal. Paul states; "For are ye not carnal: for whereas there is among you envying, and strife, and divisions, are ye not carnal and walk as men? For while one saith, I am of [the tribe of] Paul; and another, I am of [the tribe of] Apollos; are ye not carnal?" (I Corinthians 3:3-4) 'But,' one may ask, 'Can't a man find any fault in a tribe?' Obviously, since tribes are made up of people, there will always be faults to find. One does not have to have the Holy Ghost to find fault, in fact—the less Holy Ghost he has the easier it is. I have actually come to believe that there are 'fault-finding' tribes. It's amazing how tribal people like to hang around together; it's as common as nature itself. People who tend to find fault tend to also find other fault-finding people. Positive, upbeat people tend to seek out and find other positive, upbeat people: thus tribes develop. But there is still just one church; there is *one body*.

What this means is that we have to learn the meaning of the word—*tolerance*. We must learn to tolerate one another and to live with one another. We need to learn that we have different outlooks on some things, and then move on and forward.

This is true across Oneness Pentecost, within the ranks of its various organizations or non-organizational movements. It can be truthfully said that there are many tribes within the body of oneness Pentecost, but only a fool cannot recognize the positives as well as negatives in each. That is life. Only in Jesus Christ and His heaven will we find the absence of *anything negative*.

It is very unwise to allow observed negatives to blind us to obvious positives. We all simply must do our best to be what God wants us to be. I will someday have to give an account of the church I pastor. My desire is "God, whatever you have in mind for this church to be... that's what I want this church to be," in spite of the negatives.

I love the church of the living God and care what happens to it. We all realize that there are different tribes within its perimeters, and different points of view on many subjects—again that's life. Even in the local church that I pastor, I'd be shocked if I thought every single person agreed with everything I've ever said, taught, stood for, and asked people to do. To expect one hundred percent agreement on all points is to live in an imaginary world. I don't even expect that from my wife, and it's a good thing, as I would be disappointed and frustrated, and she would be worse than that.

In order for a marriage, a local church, an organization, or even a nation to function, there must be many things held in common among its participating members. "Beloved, when I gave all diligence to write unto you of the common salvation, it was needful for me to write unto you, and exhort you that ye should earnestly contend for the faith which was once delivered unto the saints." (Jude 3)

While there may be points of view we don't see-eye-to-eye on, we need to be willing, for the sake of the unity of the body, to lay down our lives for the brethren. There must be something in us that says, "Look, we may be of different tribes, but we're standing together as the church of the living God."

Certain things which may seem to be of minor importance to some, nevertheless, may be a deeply felt conviction with others. These differences may range from outlooks as to the identity of Melchisedek, to the timing of the rapture, to the non-adorning of 'wedding' rings, to proper sleeve lengths (which, by the way, in my 'tribe' is... below the elbow).

The Tunnel

Often in attempting to explain the principle of holiness, I use the example of God's church being in a tunnel. At the upward end of the tunnel there awaits a great, glorious light, while at the other downward end of the tunnel awaits an eternally dark abyss. God's people are scattered throughout the tunnel with (hopefully) all of them walking towards the light. The most important thing is the **direction that people are traveling**. If an individual—or local church—or movement—is one foot from the light, and yet turns around and keeps on going, they will eventually end up in the darkness. If someone is one foot from the darkness yet they make a turn and head for the light, they will eventually reach it. This is why the writer of Hebrews admonishes us to, "**Follow** peace with all men, and holiness, without which no man shall see the Lord." (Heb 12:14)

We must ever keep in mind that *wherever we are* in the tunnel, there is *always someone ahead of us, and someone behind us*. Our duty is to ever press onward and upward towards the light, never turning away unto darkness.

***

In the following chapters of this book I want, as much as possible, to go into detail and try to give some understanding of the necessity of God's people living a holy, separated life, concerning things that are commonly believed among us. I also want to give an answer for some standards that we have held in years past, but that some are now questioning.

I will tell you from the beginning that I don't have all the answers for all of the various tribes, be they Judah, Issachar, Zebulun, Ephraim, Manasseh, Benjamin, Dan, U.P.C., A.L.J.C., A.M.F., California, Texas, Louisiana, Florida, Kansas, Michigan, ad infinitum. But I do want to help us to understand that God has blessed us as a people, and we need to render again unto God according to the benefit that He has done unto us. (read II Chronicles 32:25)

Whatever the issue, whether it's Hollywood, television, modern technology, immorality, men's and women's hair, apparel, music, etc., whenever an attitude like Simeon's appears, God does not suffer it well. Regardless of what a person may or may not believe, if they take on an attitude that says, "I don't care what you think. I don't care what you stand for. As far as I'm concerned, this church is a bunch of fuddy-duddies. I'm going to do my thing and no one is going to tell me anything," that person is in very deep spiritual trouble, and God only knows what all other kinds of trouble awaits him.

It is intransigence, hardness, and indifference, which brings the ire of God. It is that something in the heart that says, "I am not changing for anyone or anything, my mind is made up, and if you don't like it you can lump it." This is the spirit and attitude that—unless real repentance is found—God *will* overthrow.

I've been in this way long enough to know that Issachar will grow, as men of understanding will always grow. Judah (men of praise) will grow. Some tribes may get a little weaker or smaller but that does not mean they're finished. God in His faithfulness continues to go forward. But when it comes to a 'Simeon spirit,' the blow ever remains severe.

We're not here to play church in the closing days of this dispensation. God has a *good* church but He wants to make it a *great* church. It is God's desire to show that churches in these last days who believe in holiness and righteousness can have revival and have it on a grand scale. Such churches *can* and *are* becoming *very* large and blessing the work of God throughout the world. They are starting other churches and sending forth ministers and missionaries as well as blessing the work of God financially. But there must be more men of God who will say, "We *will* rise up and vindicate the name of the Lord, and the word of God in the midst of this untoward generation."

God is a good God, and a great God, but He's also a holy God. He will work mightily, He will bless, He will move forward and He will have a people. He is also a very patient and longsuffering father towards His children. But however long-suffering God is, this must never be mistaken as a ticket for self-will and lawlessness. It is simply God's mercy saying, "I know you have failed, I know you have fallen short, but come back to me, come along with me, you can still make it—if you will but do it my way."

When the dust settles, God wants us to be there. He wants us to be standing with our hands in the air and with a host of saints ready to meet the Lord. Isaiah chapter 1 states, "The willing and the obedient shall eat the good of the land." I want to be willing and obedient. I want this church to be what God wants it to be. I want it to be what He had in mind from before the foundation of the world. Therefore, let us do our part and do what is right. We need to learn to know how to please God in every way. We need to be tender, malleable, and profitable. We need to be saved.

(Footnotes)

[1] *It is interesting to note that in the book of Revelation there are 12 tribes. Ephraim and Manasseh are still there, but Levi is also included. One tribe is missing - the tribe of Dan. God apparently eradicated them from His mentality and memory, and they are no longer represented. Yet one more sad story of the price of unrepented idolatry.*

[2] *Although all of Israel may not have been involved in this extent of nudity and lewdness (hence the death of only 3,000), they apparently were all charged as guilty for allowing this state of affairs to exist. More probably, they all dressed quickly save for the intransigent 3,000 who died not only for their folly but for their stubbornness in refusing to 'clean up their act' in the presence of godly Moses.*

Chapter Two

What a Difference a Line Can Make

This message and book began to take shape in my heart years ago as a fellow Pastor and I walked from Chula Vista, California over the international border into Tijuana, Mexico. As we crossed the actual border (which, incidentally, is made of red-colored tiles) I looked back to the San Diego/Chula Vista area of the United States, then turned south to face the city of Tijuana. I then made this statement to my friend, "What a difference a line can make."

In Tijuana the language is different, the food is different, the prices are different, the buildings are different, the automobiles are in a different condition and the traffic patterns are *very* different. What stands out to me in comparing the United States and Mexico is that the natural resources of both countries are much the same and the potential is, in many respects, equal. But due to historical circumstances and as well as religious hierarchy, time has worked vast differences between these two nations. When you step across that line you step into another world. I don't blame the people in Mexico who attempt to cross the border and enter the United States. I assure you that if I lived there, and saw a chance to better my family's living conditions by fleeing to America, I would by all means do so.

The most telling and emotional moment for me was upon our return to the U.S. As we walked back across the line I looked off to my right, at a seemingly endless chain-link fence. Off in the distance stood a young man gripping the fence, staring north. There was no one on the north side of the fence looking south. I have never, in all of my visits to Mexico, seen anyone on the north side gaze longingly towards the south. Anyone I have ever seen holding that fence was on the south side wanting, without a doubt, to cross the border, northward. Though I sincerely hope that the boy made it, I would to God that people were as hungry to get into Heaven as they are to get into the United States of America.

The Importance of Lines

History is replete with examples showing the importance of lines. In 1836 William Travis, in a vast area known as Tejas (now Texas), drew a line in the sand. He then said, 'Everyone who is willing to remain here and fight, step forward.' All 156 men stepped forward, save one man who escaped and lived to tell the story of the Alamo. The line those men crossed made the difference between their own life and death, and a vast difference in the history of Texas.

By late August of 1939, Germany had amassed thousands of troops at their border with Poland. Everyone knew they were there and why they were there, although no declaration of war had been made. Great Britain and France had a treaty with Poland stating that war would be declared on Germany if it ever crossed that border in aggression. It was a line of demarcation. Germany crossed the line on September 1, 1939 and World War II began. Before it ended the nations of the world would experience over 50 million casualties.

Government officials deal with lines on a daily basis. I live in the County of San Bernardino, California, and am under county ordinances. But if I cross the street at the end of my block I am also in the City of Rialto, and under its codes and laws. It does make a difference. For one thing, the Sheriff's Department handles problems on my side of the line and the Rialto Police Department handles problems on the other side of the line.

The Federal Bureau of Investigation deals with interstate lines. The FBI is not interested in some crimes unless in the process of committing it, or fleeing, they cross a state line. The CIA deals with international lines. Every day, officers around the world in cities, counties, states and nations work within lines and borders. A line can make a vast difference in the kingdom of men as well as in the kingdom of God.

Lines in Egypt

"And the Lord gave the people favor in the sight of the Egyptians. Moreover the man Moses was very great in the land of Egypt, in the sight of Pharaoh's servants and in the sight of the people. And Moses said, thus saith the Lord, about **midnight**, will I go out in the midst of **Egypt** and all the **firstborn** in the land of Egypt shall die from the firstborn of Pharaoh that sitteth upon his throne. Even unto the firstborn of the maidservant that is behind the mill and all the firstborn of beast. There shall be a great cry throughout all the land of Egypt ; such as there was none like it nor shall be like it any more. But against any of the **children of Israel** shall not a dog move his tongue against man or beast that you may know how the Lord doth put a difference between the Egyptian and Israel. And all these thy servants shall come down unto me and bow down themselves unto me saying get thee out, and all the people that follow thee after thee will I go out. And He went out from Pharaoh in great anger. And the Lord said unto Moses, Pharaoh shall not hearken unto you that my wonders may be multiplied in the land of Egypt. And Moses and Aaron did all these wonders before Pharaoh and the Lord hardened Pharaoh's heart that he would not let the children of Israel go out of the land." (Exodus 11:3-10)

"Now all these things happened unto them for example and they are written for our admonition upon whom the ends of the world are come." (I Corinthians 10:11)

In this passage from Exodus, God speaks through Moses to tell Pharaoh that some lines are about to be drawn in Egypt. He said that at "about midnight" the angel would come; that is a *time line* of demarcation. Midnight is not in the morning, nor at sunset, but at the darkest time of the night. At midnight God was going to draw a line in the sands of time that would never be forgotten.

The angel was to go through the length and breadth of Egypt. He was not to go into the nations that lay to the south or to the west. He was not to go to the Bedouins who lived in the Sinai Peninsula, nor was he to go north and touch anyone who was in a ship on the Mediterranean Sea. The death angel was to *stop at the borders* that defined and separated Egypt from the rest of the world. God was recognizing lines.

The angel was going to every house that did not have *blood* painted on the doorpost. If you lived in Egypt, no matter what your nationality was, if you did not desire the death angel to visit your house, then you must take a lamb without spot, the firstborn of the flock, and slay him. The blood of any other creature was not acceptable as God drew a line between what He would accept as sacrifice and what He would not. Then you were to take a hyssop plant, dip it into the blood of the lamb, and put it on the sides and top of the doors of your house. This was a line that marked the difference between life and death.

If the blood was not on the doorpost when midnight came, then another line was drawn. The death angel did not slay fathers or mothers, even though they were the ones at fault for not obeying Moses, but he slew *the firstborn* of every household in Egypt. Even the firstborn of every animal was slain that night. When time ran out for Egypt, those who had failed to draw the line let out a great cry. The Bible states there was weeping and wailing that went up in Egypt such as had never been heard before, or since.

We see therefore that God recognized several variously drawn lines. He dealt with both Israel and Egypt through lines, honored them and ministered through a multiplicity of such lines. God put a difference between those who were His people and those who were not. Take note that God did not send an angel *to draw* the line of blood—that was the people's responsibility. He sent an angel to recognize and honor the lines that *were drawn*. Any person who did not have enough faith to act upon the words of Moses suffered the consequences.

These were the first lines drawn for the nation of Israel, but they were by no means the last.

In the Wilderness

In I Corinthians 10 Paul wrote of the Israelites who came out of Egypt. They went through the Red Sea and were baptized unto Moses; a prototype of baptism unto Jesus Christ. Their exodus from Egypt was a type of repentance. They were led forth by the glory cloud in the daytime, which became a pillar of fire by night; this being a type of the New Testament Holy Ghost experience. Everything that happened to these people was meant to be an example to the New Testament church of today that we might learn invaluable lessons in order to please God and see our souls saved. Some may say, "That is Old Testament and it's not for the church today." Our answer is, "What scriptures do you think the first church used? The only scriptures they had were the Old Testament." (I actually prefer the term 'First' Testament but use 'Old' for clarity's sake). Every reference point they had was Old Testament. All teachings that were given them were based on the bedrock of the Old Testament.

When the Israelites arrived in the wilderness God gave them commandments concerning the tabernacle that they were to erect in their midst. He did so because He desired to come and dwell with them. They were given dimensions for the outer court, for the length and breadth of the tabernacle, for the holy place and for the Holy of Holies. God told Moses after he received these instructions, "According to all that I show thee, after the pattern of the tabernacle...even so shall ye make it." (Exodus 25:9) Moses was to put the lines exactly where God said they should be placed.

Lines of Law

God began teaching them, giving them His laws, and thus drawing more lines. When Moses came down from Sinai, God began the process of separating these Israelites from all other peoples who were on the face of the earth. He let them know the exact boundaries that would constitute their nation. They were going to be separated geographically, but more importantly, they were going to be separated spiritually, morally and theologically from the other nations of the world. This meant that they would also be separated mentally and emotionally. God even went so far as to separate them financially, showing that the economics of God's people is unlike the systems of the world.

God separated His people because He wanted them to be His peculiar treasure, and "He is the same yesterday, today and forever." (Hebrews 13:8) God does not change, He is still going to have a people. His people are not going to believe like the world, think like the world, look like the world, live like the world or give like the world. He wants us to be a peculiar people—His treasure. That is why He states in Exodus 19:5, "Now therefore, if you will obey my voice, indeed and keep my covenant, then ye shall be a peculiar treasure [peculiar to the world but cherished by God] above all people, for all the earth is mine. And ye shall be unto me a kingdom of priests and a holy nation. These are the words which thou shalt speak unto the children of Israel."

It is a good feeling if your boss appreciates you so much that he says of you, "That employee is a treasure." It is nice to be a treasure to your family, school, or community. But if I am going to be a treasure to anyone, I want to be a treasure to God. There is something intrinsic in our nature—both Holy Ghost nature and human nature—that compels us to take care of a treasure—unless of course we are a fool. God is not foolish and because we are a treasure to Him He is going to take care of us. Whatever must be done to be pleasing in His sight we must do, by the grace of God, that we might be one of His treasures.

The Vineyard and the Fence

The story of God's relationship with His treasure, Israel, is told many times in the Word of the Lord, from different outlooks and various angles. One of the most beautiful and poetic renditions is found in the book of Isaiah, chapter 5 and verse 1:

"Now will I sing to my wellbeloved a song of my beloved touching his vineyard. My beloved hath a vineyard in a very fruitful hill. And he fenced it, and gathered out the stones thereof, and planted it with the choicest vine, and built a tower in the midst of it, and also made a winepress therein: and he looked that it should bring forth grapes."

While this stanza is speaking of Israel, it also speaks to us today.

He labored in the vineyard, and *"gathered out the stones thereof."* When God places a soul in His vineyard, He uses three main avenues of grace to work in that life and remove the 'stumbling stones of offense': the Word of God, the Spirit of God, and the man of God. It should be our desire to be tenderhearted before God, yielding always to Him that He can *gather out the stones*—the hard places of our spirit.

He planted it with the choicest vine. Jesus said, "I am the true vine." Jesus Himself is planted in our innermost being when we receive Him in the new birth, Holy Ghost experience. (read Colossians 1:27 and John 14:17-18)

He put a tower in the midst of it. "The name of the Lord is a strong tower: the righteous run into it, and is safe." (Proverbs 18:10) We receive His name in baptism and are safe.

He put a winepress therein. Whatever our needs are, they can be met by a deep experience *with* and spiritual grasp *of* God. Just as the winepress was within the midst of the garden (so that they need not go elsewhere) so are our answers not far from any one of us. This new wine we have received is the Spirit of Almighty God and it dwells—within us.

But please note; **of all things that God did in His vineyard, the very first thing He did was to—*fence it.*** Why did He fence the vineyard? Did He fear that it would run off? As a vineyard cannot *'run away,'* God fenced it for two main reasons:

1. For protective or defensive purposes. The word 'defense' comes literally from the word 'fence.'

2. To declare His ownership. 'This vineyard *is mine* and I'm going to protect it.' What He did was draw a line—and He drew it with His law.

In Deuteronomy 4:1-2 it says, "Now therefore hearken, O Israel, unto the statutes and unto the judgments, which I teach you, for to do them, that ye may live, and go in and possess the land which the Lord God of your fathers giveth you. Ye shall not add unto the word which I command you, neither shall be diminish ought from it, that ye may keep the commandments of the Lord your God which I command you." Verses 5 - 9 state, "Behold, I have taught you statutes and judgments, even as the Lord my God commanded me, that you should do so in the land whither ye go to possess it."

The first thing God did when He brought Israel out was to begin teaching them statutes. In so doing He was putting up a fence. He was gathering out stones and placing a productive vine in their place.

"Keep therefore and do them; for this is your wisdom and your understanding in the sight of the nations, which shall hear all these statutes, and say, Surely this great nation is a wise and understanding people. For what nation is there so great, who hath God so nigh unto them, as the Lord our God is in all things that we call upon him for? And what nation is there so great, that hath statutes and judgments so righteous as all this law, which I set before you this day? Only take heed to thyself, and keep thy soul diligently, lest thou forget the things which thine eyes have seen, and lest they depart from thy heart all the day of thy life; but teach thy sons, and thy sons' sons." (Deuteronomy 4:6-9)

This "fence" was not just for that generation, but for their children and their children's children.

Fighting For Our Children

The ruling class of the ancient city-state of Sparta in Greece, have gone down in history as some of the world's greatest, most disciplined, most feared warriors. While the 'Spartans' were by no means the only warring people of ancient Greece, these men were in a class all of their own. The most famous example of this was seen when Xerxes, king of Persia sought to invade Greece in 480 B.C. He came with an army of 2 million men and had to bring them through a bottlenecked area known as Thermopylae. To buy time for Greece to get its military act together, the various city-states amassed a 4,000-man force to stop or at least impede the Persians at this strategically vulnerable region. The cream of this fighting force was 300 hand-picked Spartans. After a week of unbelievably fierce fighting, approximately 1,200 Greeks escaped to fight again. The vast majority of those who remained were Spartans. The Spartan force at Thermopylae was ultimately slain to a man, but not before killing over 20,000 Persians.

This feat was accomplished only by fierce tenacity and years of incredible in-depth training and discipline. From their earliest years, Spartan boys were taught that when they were engaged in battle they were not just fighting for themselves, they were fighting for their gods (pagan though they were), for their children, and for their children's children. *They were fighting for all the unborn generations that would never exist if they failed.* They understood that a tremendous responsibility rested upon their shoulders.

If the men of Sparta could grasp that concept for a temporal city-state, how much more should we—of this heavenly kingdom—realize that when we "contend for the faith once delivered to the saints" (Jude 3) we are not fighting just for our own preservation. We are fighting for the church, for our children and for our children's children. *If the Lord should tarry, we are fighting for a thousand generations.*

God's message to Israel was, 'Place these laws in your heart, get them in your soul, in your mind, and in your spirit. Don't let them drift away or slip, because they are your wisdom and understanding. The keeping of these laws is what makes you a peculiar treasure unto me.' Whenever Israel disobeyed these laws, they became just like—and no better than the nations that God had thrust out before them. Their rebellion caused God to be at enmity with them, and even the heathen had no use for them. Israel became a laughing-stock. Although God had set them apart for Himself, for His name, and for His glory, God's people became a 'joke'—and a bad one at that.

I do not want the church that I pastor, or any church for that matter, to become a joke in the sight of the Angels or this world. Whatever God had in mind for His church to be, let us fulfill that. This will only be accomplished by a thorough application of our lives, homes and churches to the principles and precepts of God's word.

Lines and Precepts

God's lines are direct, unequivocal commandments. A 'precept' however is different; by definition it is 'a principal intended as a general rule of action or conduct or procedure.' Many scriptures God gives us are plainly spoken, easily understood, 'black and white' commandments. Acts 2:38 contains a direct commandment to those who are honest-hearted and unsullied by the traditions of men. There are other scriptures that are given as precepts, or principles, such as honesty, integrity, generosity, mercy, love, faithfulness and hundreds more.

How does God's Word deliver to us His precepts and principles? In the book of Isaiah chapter 28 and verse 9 we read, "Whom shall he teach knowledge? And whom shall be make to understand doctrine? Them that are weaned from the milk, and drawn from the breasts. For precept must be upon precept, precept upon precept; line upon line, line upon line; here a little and there a little."

As an example let us look at the doctrine of water baptism. There is no one chapter that tells us everything we need to know about the subject. Rather, from Genesis to Revelation it is 'here a line and there a line, here a precept and there a precept.' The types and metaphors that depict baptism are found 'here and there' all the way through scripture. It begins in Genesis chapter 1 vs. 6 with the 'separation of the waters.' Moving to Genesis chapter 6, we read of Noah's ark and the flood that washed away a sinful world. Simon Peter refers to this in his second epistle; 3:20-21, "...Few, that is, eight souls were saved by water. The like figure where unto even baptism doth also now save us..."

Another metaphor concerning baptism is seen when the children of Israel crossed through the parted waters of the Red Sea. When the Egyptian army assayed to do so they were drowned. This is symbolic of sin being washed away, and paves the way for Paul's teaching in I Corinthians chapter 10 that the children of Israel "...were baptized unto Moses...."

Many more references to baptism are taught to us "here a little and there a little." In Mark 16:16, "He that believeth and is baptized shall be saved; but he that believeth not shall be damned." In Acts 8:12 and vs. 16 Philip baptized in the Name of the Lord Jesus. In Acts 10:48 Peter commanded the newly-filled Holy Ghost believers of Cornelius' house to be baptized in the Name of the Lord. In chapter 19 the believers at Ephesus had already been baptized unto John's baptism. But they were re-baptized in the Name of the Lord Jesus at the preaching of the Apostle Paul. Scattered throughout scripture, a little here, and a little there, we see the doctrine of baptism displayed.

In Isaiah 28:9 God gives another precept. "For with stammering lips and another tongue will he speak to this people. To whom he said, This is the rest wherewith ye may cause the weary to rest; and this is the refreshing; yet they would not hear." He is speaking of a precept concerning a rest for His people: a Sabbath. It is important for us to understand that when a person receives the gift of the Holy Ghost they are receiving the Sabbath experience. They receive rest to their souls.

How does one know when they have received the Holy Ghost? As they call upon the Lord Jesus and worship Him with a repentant heart, the Spirit of God will fall. [If the repented individual has yet to be baptized in Jesus Name he can *most assuredly* expect the Spirit to fall as he comes up out of the water] Their lips and tongue will begin to 'stammer,' and as they release themselves in faith to God, He takes over and begins to speak through them in another tongue (language) that they have never learned, be it a language of men or of angels.

This is all accomplished as the Spirit gives the utterance. (Acts 2:1-4) Paul states that it is "...not I, but Christ that worketh in me." (Gal. 2:20) It is the grace of God. We thank God for the Holy Ghost experience.

Another precept was given when God drew the lines of the tabernacle. When one entered into the tabernacle the first item seen was the brazen altar. There was blood at the altar; that is where the priest offered up the sacrifice. They then moved on to the brazen laver to "wash with water that they die not." (Exodus 30:20) From there they entered into the holy place, which is indicative of the Holy Ghost, the presence of Almighty God.

The death at the altar is symbolic of our death to our sins by way of repentance. The washing at the laver is a type of baptism. The entering into the Holy Place is a metaphor of entering into the Holy Ghost. In Acts 2:38, on the Day of Pentecost, Peter brings all of these beautiful truths together in the first message preached in this dispensation of Grace, "Then Peter said unto the, Repent, and be baptized every one of you in the name of Jesus Christ for the remission of sins, and ye shall receive the gift of the Holy Ghost."

God made sure that no one verse, no one chapter, would cover it all. Instead, cardinal doctrines are spelled out in lines and precepts given throughout the body of scripture, 'here a little and there a little.'

But why did God do it that way? Why didn't He just give one doctrine in this chapter (or book) and another doctrine in the next—as in the manner of a textbook? For one thing, He is not a college professor—He is God. Why did He give it here a little, there a little? The startling answer is found in the 13th verse of Isaiah 28; "That they might go and fall backward and be broken and snared and taken."

He sets forth His doctrine in this scattered manner in order that a person void of *an honest heart* will not see truth or enter the portals of glory. God authored His Word in such a way that if someone does not want to see truth, they can figure out a way not to. If one doesn't want to be honest, it's possible to finagle a way to be dishonest. Scripture is presented in a manner that those who *do enter* are going to do so both honestly and scripturally, in spite of every opportunity *not* to do so.

If we make it to Heaven it will be that, among other things, we recognized that this *is* God's 'modus operandi,' his mode of operation. This *is the way* He gives doctrine, understanding and knowledge. He has simply chosen it to be so.

The Mount and its Boundaries

At Mount Sinai in the wilderness Moses went up for 40 days and nights, neither eating nor drinking, sustained only by the presence of God. It was there that God gave him the Ten Commandments. These commandments were clear lines of demarcation that separated Israel from the other nations about them.

Before Moses went up, God told him in Exodus 19:10-11, "And the Lord said unto Moses, Go unto the people, and sanctify them to day and to morrow, and let them wash their clothes, and be ready against the third day; for the third day the Lord will come down in the sight of all the people upon mount Sinai. And thou shalt set bounds unto the people round about, saying, Take heed to yourselves, that ye go not up into the mount, or touch the border of it: whosoever toucheth the mount shall be surely put to death."

There are interesting things to note here. First, it was Moses job to set bounds for the people about the mountain (Exodus 19:15).

But where does a mountain start? There is no manual or guidebook that states where a mountain stops or starts. But as God was going to speak directly to the people, He expected Moses to set the bounds as well as command Israel to sanctify themselves. Obviously, *Moses had to decide* where to set the boundary—it was his responsibility. God did not tell him *where* to set it, He simply told him to set it.

The second item to note is that if anyone broke through the border that Moses set, be they man or beast, it was the responsibility of the congregation to see that the offender was stoned or thrust through with a dart. God honored the line that Moses drew and expected His people to do the same.

Understand that when God came down onto this mount, unimaginable glory and power was revealed. The Bible tells us in both Exodus and Hebrews that the earth itself trembled. The entire mountain quaked from the presence of Almighty God, and was engulfed by a dark cloud. Out of this cloud came great thunders, lightnings, and the sound of a mass of heavenly trumpets. Above all these terrifying sounds was the *utterly overpowering voice of God* Himself. It was a scene of such magnitude and awe that Moses said, "I myself exceedingly fear and quake."

The terrified Israelites begged Moses to stop God's audible speaking, promising; 'Moses, if you'll go up into the mount, listen to Him, and come back, anything He tells you to do we will obey. But we cannot endure this intense glory, this direct voice of God.' And that is exactly what Moses did.

Imagine the glory, the shaking, the thunder, the lightning, the sound of trumpets and the voice of God. One would think that with that much power, that much quaking and fear, that much of the awesome presence of God, that if someone were to break through and touch the mount, the glory of God *itself* would instantly kill them. But God said that He was not going to do it. He commanded them, 'If somebody touches the mount, *you* kill them. *You* stone them. *You* thrust them with a dart.' It was *the congregation's responsibility* to protect the mount and the presence of God. What God was ultimately saying is;

'I am not going to protect my glory. If it is going to be protected at all, it is up to the people to do it.'

This is one reason why numbers of churches do not have the glory of God in their midst; they don't care enough about it to protect it. God's attitude is, 'If it isn't important enough to you to protect it, I will simply remove it. I will find someone who *is* willing to protect it and who *does* care, who *does* love me, who *does* want my laws. I will find someone who *wants* to please me. If you don't care about my glory, there will be someone, somewhere, who will.'

For this reason God said to Moses—at the provocation at Kadesh Barnea—"But as truly as I live, all the earth shall be filled with the glory of the LORD." (Num 14:21)

God will see to it. If that people and that generation did not value His glory, there was coming a people who will. He will gather them from every generation, from all centuries, from every nation, kindred and tongue. They are going to make up His bride. They are going to be a people who love Him and are willing to walk within the bounds of His word. They will allow Him to remove the stones of misconception. They will take on His name and love it. They will receive His Spirit and walk in it. They will love His glory and protect it. They will do that which is right in His sight.

They will be willing to keep the fences.

Phinehas and the Glory

Let's return to Balak, the king of Moab, and the lewd Moabite women. Moab had offered the meat up to their idols and afterwards offered it to Israel. The Israelites, after filling their bellies and searing their consciences in the process, fell immediately into the next thing Moab offered—lust and fornication. This so incensed God that He sent a plague into their midst. Moses, Joshua and the elders fled to the tabernacle, threw dust into the air and cried out to God. Zimri the Simeonite stood at the door of the tabernacle with his Moabite girlfriend on his arm, laughing and mocking at the godly mourners. He then took the hussy into his tent while the elders cried and the plague rolled on.

But there was someone in that generation and congregation who loved the glory of God. His name was Phinehas, of the tribe of Levi, Simeon's old running partner. This righteous man took a spear, entered Zimri's tent and slew both Zimri and his partner in lust. And the instant they died—*the plague stopped.*

God recognized that Phinehas greatly valued His glory and was willing to protect it. Phinehas didn't hesitate to destroy a profane, vile, bold, impudent spirit that sneered at sanctity and brazenly defiled God's glory.

The deeds of Zimri declared, 'I'm going to do my own thing and I don't care what God says. I don't care where His lines are or what His precepts declare; it doesn't matter to me. I do what I want and have no regrets or remorse.'

However, God's reply is, 'Go ahead. I only want people who are honest and sincere anyway. But you are *not* going to do your thing here in my presence, within the bounds of my people who I have set apart for my name's sake—and my glory remain. If you do *your thing*, and no one cares enough to rise up and do something about it, then I will remove myself and my glory.'

Thank God for Phinehas.

***

Sometimes people ask their pastor, "Why don't you just make people do right?" My answer is, "Why doesn't God make people do right? He is the omnipotent one, not me." I cannot *force* anyone to do right. I can only try to influence them using weapons of spiritual warfare—which are not carnal.

However… if someone in the congregation utterly refuses to obey God and takes on a defiant, profane spirit against His Holiness, as pastor I cannot allow them to hold office or be used in the church. If it continues after I have "in meekness instructed those that oppose themselves, that God peradventure might grant them repentance to the acknowledgment of the truth," (II Timothy 2:25) and after having gone through the process prescribed in Matthew 18:15-17, then I must ask (or tell) them to leave. I may even have to "deliver such an one unto Satan for the destruction of the flesh, that the spirit may [possibly] be saved in the day of the Lord Jesus." (I Corinthians 5:5) And I have—when pressed—had to do all of these things.

But again, why doesn't God just make people do right? Because He is the creator of the free moral agency of man. He only wants people who are willing and obedient. (read Isaiah 1:19) He desires those who desire Him, who will say; "As for me and my house, we are going to walk in the grace, truth and goodness of God."

Mumbles and the "Treasure Map"

Several years ago while pastoring on the central coast of California, our church was trying to get into the local state prison facility to hold services. While the Protestant chaplain was a very good man to work with, and was doing his best to help us get in, there were other prison officials working very hard to keep us out.

Part of the process in order to receive final approval was for me, as pastor, to be placed in a little room with several convicts, where we discussed theological matters. These sessions took place over the course of a few weeks and there was always a member of the Chaplains staff present. I came to realize that this was a proving ground to observe how I would react to the various prisoners and issues.

One day they brought into our group a man called 'Mumbles.' Mumbles was a brilliant but thoroughly confused human being. His theology was a jumble of various weird philosophies with just enough scripture thrown in to make him spiritually dangerous. He fiercely loved to fiercely argue his skewed points of view. On this day Mumbles and a couple of his disciples went after me with a vengeance. Apparently, Mumbles was somewhat familiar with Oneness Apostolics, despised them, and thought this a good time to 'get his pound of flesh.' Everyone was watching to see how I would react to the onslaught.

Statements were made like, "Who do these people think they are, to say 'they're the only ones who have the truth?' Who do these people think they are, to say 'there is only one way to be saved?' God has many avenues and roads to Heaven." Mumbles monologue went on in this vein for about 45 minutes. I prayed under my breath that God would help me and give me wisdom. Thankfully… He did.

I finally said to Mumbles and his fellow listeners, "I want to tell you a story of a man who had endless riches. Being a kind, generous and righteous man, He wanted to share these riches with people who were worthy, because they were honest with themselves, with each other, and with him."

"So he gave them a treasure map to tell them how to get to the treasure from wherever they might be living throughout the whole world. This map was written so that in order to follow it, you must possess an honest heart and a deep desire to seek after the treasure. You also had to have a humble heart that would say, 'Not my will but thy will be done."

"Now Mumbles, God is obviously the endlessly rich man, the Bible is the treasure map and the Kingdom of Heaven is the treasure. Wherever you are on the face of the earth, you can find the treasure because it is not in a geographical location. It is not found at the intersection of a certain latitude and longitude. It is in a spiritual location, at the point where Spirit and Truth meet. But in order to find it you have to be very, very honest." I then explained God's method of giving doctrine and knowledge by lines and precepts; "here a little and there a little."

Then I said, "But Mumbles, God did not put us here to fight and argue over the treasure map. He put us here to follow His map—the Bible. So I'm following it the best I can. I'm following it like Jesus said to, as well as Simon Peter, the Apostle Paul and all the other writers that God used to give it. I am striving to fulfill the teachings of Jesus, and to obey the types, patterns, lines and precepts; get to Heaven and take as many people with me as I can."

Mumbles responded, "How do you know I'm not going to Heaven? I *obey an inner voice* that speaks to me. That is all that anyone has to do, simply obey the inner voice that is in each of us and it will get us to heaven."

"Well, Mumbles," I said, "Time will tell if your inner voice will get you to heaven or not. But I do have one question for you; did obeying your inner voice get you into this prison?"

His 'disciples' looked at him closely and waited for his answer while Mumbles looked rather chagrined, but nevertheless replied, "I obey the voice, and the voice will get me into Heaven."

I answered, "But obeying these 'inner voices' can be somewhat risky. What if *my inner voice* tells me to kill you? Should I listen to that voice, or should I listen to the voice of God as it is found in this Bible?"

Mumbles' answer to that query made no more sense than anything else he said, but the next day I received official notice that we had been accepted to come to the facility and minister. They must have figured that if I could get past Mumbles I could get past anyone.

***

Again, God wrote and gave the world His word (His Treasure Map) in such a way that if someone wants to make it, they can. *But they have to have an honest heart.* He did not put His word here for people to fight over it—but to obey it. When the disciples of Jesus asked Him what they ought to do about the scribes and Pharisees— the hypocrites of their day—His answer was, "Let them alone. They be blind leaders of the blind." (Matthew 15:14)

In the closing days of this dispensation we must do our best to lift up the truth, love, righteousness and holiness of our Lord and Savior, Jesus Christ. In so doing we find ourselves at war with the endtime forces of Hell. It is a fight, but fight on we will.

"For though we walk in the flesh, we do not war after the flesh: (For the weapons of our warfare are not carnal, but mighty through God to the pulling down of strong holds;) Casting down imaginations, and every high thing that exalteth itself against the knowledge of God, and bringing into captivity every thought to the obedience of Christ." (2 Cor. 10:3-5)

We are fighting not just for God and ourselves, but we are fighting for the church, our children and our children's children. We must have His glory, His presence and His power. We must have His grace; we need His goodness; we need the mind of His spirit. We long to possess all the spiritual promise land that He wants us to have. In order to accomplish this we need God, and we need His lines and precepts.

Chapter Three

The Glory and the Man of God

Years ago I pastored a precious little lady in Oklahoma named Edith Floyd. Her husband, David Lee Floyd, had received the Holy Ghost in 1910 and had, along with Charles Smith, taken the message of baptism in Jesus' name to the Elton Bible Conference in Louisiana in 1915. Dear Sister Floyd couldn't sing; to be honest, she couldn't carry a tune in a bushel basket. Her voice creaked and croaked and cracked and was not enjoyable to listen to. It didn't matter if the musicians played well or not, because she always cut her own path anyway. But whenever the musicians got the idea that they were indispensable and church couldn't go on without them, I would get Sister Floyd by the hand and bring her up to the platform.

I felt safe in doing this for the following reason; every time she opened her mouth to sing the glory of God fell. The saints would lift their hands, and soon there would be praying, shouting or crying. The presence of God grew stronger and stronger as she creaked and croaked her way through her song. Almost without fail visitors would ask; "What was that I felt when that old lady sang?"

No one ever complimented her ability, but they did compliment how God honored her effort. She didn't sing every service or every week; I only had her sing maybe two or three times a year. But she was a good reminder that God blesses availability and consecration more than He blesses ability alone.

Money cannot buy His glory. Ability cannot bring it down. It will not manifest itself just because we think it's a good idea. There has to be something in the hearts of God's people that so loves, so appreciates and so desires it, that God responds by pouring it into their midst. There must be something in the hearts of God's people that they would defend His glory, if need be, to the death.

A god without Glory

While Moses was up on Mount Sinai God spoke to him and said; "Go, get thee down; for thy people, which thou broughtest out of the land of Egypt, have corrupted themselves." (Ex 32:7)

Just 40 days earlier the glory had been at the bottom of the mount. The people had begged Moses to go and hear from God himself, as the sheer, raw presence and power of God was too much for them. Now, only 40 days later their awe had completely vanished, and their saying to Aaron was; "Up, make us gods, which shall go before us; for as for this Moses, the man that brought us up out of the land of Egypt, we wot not what is become of him." (Ex 32:1) So Aaron took their jewelry, which they had collected from the Egyptians, and from this jewelry he fashioned a golden calf and declared, "These be thy gods, O Israel..." (Exod. 32:4) At that point the people stripped off their clothes and began to dance and play around the golden calf.

While they carried on like ignorant pagans, God told Moses to get down from the mount because the people had corrupted themselves. Joshua, coming down with Moses, thought he heard the "Noise of war in the camp." (Exodus 32:17) Upon further consideration he said, "It is not the voice of them that shout for mastery, neither is it the voice of them that cry for being overcome: but the noise of them that sing do I hear." (verse 18) These holy men of God came down from the mount and the presence of God—to behold a backslidden congregation.

Why in the world would a people—who had beheld such glory that it caused the entire mountain to shake—made lightning and thunder appear—and brought the blast of heavenly trumpets—trade that experience, power and splendor… *for an idol made of gold*? They had witnessed the creation of this "god" by Aaron and therefore knew the source of its being. This god possessed no aura, no power and no glory. It had not a hint of life. It could neither hear prayers nor answer them. It couldn't make a twig shake, let alone a mountain. It couldn't bring thunder, lightning, or produce the sound of a single earthly trumpet. Again, how could a people who had seen *so much*, been *so blessed* and *received such a powerful deliverance* by Jehovah God—trade such glory and splendor—for a speechless and lifeless god—in such a short period of time?

The god of No Demands

"For they preferred a statue of an ox that eats grass, to the glorious presence of God himself." (Psalm 106:19-20) (Tay)

"They exchanged the glory of God for the disgrace of idols." (Hosea 4:7) (Tay)

The answer is, that *a golden calf asks nothing*. It makes no demands; you can live any way you want, talk any way you want, and go anywhere you want. You can even take your clothes off and dance around in its very presence naked if you have a mind to. In this regard there is no comparison between the golden calf and the God of Glory.

As soon as the God of Glory began speaking, He began making demands. The first thing He said was, "Thou shalt have no other gods before me." *God's glory makes demands on those who are allowed to have it in their midst.*

Benjamin Disraeli once said; "Life is nothing but a series of negotiations," or in other words, "everything in life is a trade-off." To have the glory requires a trade-off of our will for God's will, His word over our ways.

What a glorious trade-off! We are seemingly so insignificant compared to this vast universe. Yet if we will but love and serve Him with all our heart, the great God and Creator will love us in kind, even to the same degree that the Father loved the Son, or as *the Divinity loved the humanity; the Spirit loved the flesh.* "As the Father hath loved me, so have I loved you..." (John 15:9)

Who can possibly begin to comprehend the depths of *that* love? I cite but two of the many verses that give us insight into 'that love. and 'that relationship': "To whit, that God was **in Christ**, reconciling the world **unto himself**...." (II Corinthians 5:19) and, "Hereby perceive we the love of God, in that **He** laid down **His life** for us...." (I John 3:16) While everything in life is a trade-off, this surely is the most wonderful exchange of all: His love and care for our love and obedience. This 'trade off' is found (in different terminology) in Isaiah 61:3 where God gives "...beauty for ashes, the oil of joy for mourning, the garment of praise for the spirit of heaviness."

I have been privileged to preach across America and around the world and have witnessed that the glory falls when people are living in *close* accordance with God's word. It descends among people whose lives declare, "As for me and my house, we will serve God faithfully. I am going to do what He desires. I'm going to live the way He wants me to live, and worship Him from my heart accordingly." When we live and worship Him in spirit and in truth, we are protecting the glory of God. Again, God will not protect it for us—He leaves that up to us.

In Defense of the Glory

"Be strong and of a good courage; for unto this people shalt thou divide for an inheritance the land, which I sware unto their fathers to give them. Only be thou strong and very courageous, that thou **mayest observe to do accordingly to all the law**, which Moses my servant commanded thee; **turn not from it to the right hand or to the left**, that thou **mayest prosper** whithersoever thou goest. This book of the law shall not depart out of thy mouth; but thou shalt meditate therein day and night, that thou mayest **observe to do according to all that is written therein**; for **then thou shalt make thy way prosperous, and then thou shalt have good success.** Have not I commanded thee? Be strong and of a good courage; be not afraid, neither be thou dismayed; for the Lord thy God is with thee whithersoever thou goest; Then Joshua commanded the officers of the people, saying, Pass through the host, and command the people, saying, prepare you victuals; for within three days ye shall pass over this Jordan, to go in to possess the land, which the Lord your God giveth you to possess it" (Joshua 1:6-11).

God was about to give His people the land that He swore He would give unto their father Abraham. God promised that He would be with them and that they would see His victory and glory. Thus Israel began passing through the land experiencing tremendous victories, even overcoming the great walled city of Jericho.

They finally came to a small city called Ai. The fighting men said to Joshua that there was no point in turning aside the whole vast assembly in order to conquer such a minute city. Only 3,000 men should be sent to take Ai, while the rest of the assembly continued to go forward. This sounded like good reasoning to Joshua, so he sent this small portion of the army on to what seemed like certain victory.

They attacked the city—but were smitten and repelled. Thirty-six Israelites were killed and Israel was stunned. The victors over great Jericho were defeated before little Ai. The subdued Israeli army returned to the camp for a session of weeping and wailing.

"And Joshua rent his clothes, and fell to the earth upon his face before the ark of the Lord until the eventide, he and the elders of Israel, and put dust upon their heads. And Joshua said, Alas, O Lord God, wherefore hast thou at all brought this people over Jordan to deliver us into the hand of the Amorites, to destroy us? Would to God we had been content, and dwelt on the other side Jordan!" (Joshua 7:6-7) Verses 10 and 11 go on to say, "And the Lord said unto Joshua, Get thee up; wherefore liest thou thus upon thy face? Israel hath sinned...."

God let Joshua know that the problem was not with God, but with Israel. "And they have also transgressed my covenant which I commanded them: for they have even taken of the accursed thing, and have also stolen, and dissembled also, and they put it even among their own stuff. Therefore the children of Israel could not stand before their enemies, but turned their backs before their enemies, because they were accursed." God further states, "Neither will I be with you anymore except ye destroy the accursed from among you." (Joshua 7:12)

God gave this last pronouncement in spite of the precious promises already made to Israel. This teaches us that sin committed by God's people does indeed have the power to forestall, if not negate, the promises of God. That He would go so far as to say, "**Neither will I be with you anymore** except ye destroy the accursed from among you," ought to give us pause for great consideration.

Another crucial point is that only *one man* in that vast congregation had sinned. During the battle of Jericho, a man named Achan took a Babylonish garment, 200 shekels of silver and a wedge of gold and hid them in his tent. This defied the commandment of God to consecrate all the goods of that city to Him. Achan's disobedience and covetousness led to the defeat of Israel in the battle of Ai. Consistent victory *from* God depends upon consistent obedience *to* God.

Through this episode, God is speaking to His people in all generations; 'If you want my victorious glory to be with you, you must take care of it by keeping my commandments.' If His commandments are not honored, God will back away from His people and their dilemmas. Before Israel could be returned to the realm of glory and victory, Achan—his immediate family—his oxen—asses—sheep—tents—the Babylonish garment—the silver—and the gold—*all had to be destroyed.* God will find out how much His victory and glory really means to us. There are times in life when we are called upon to make excruciatingly painful but unbelievably important decisions. And even if dealing with friends or family, we must choose God— His glory and victory, over the way of Achan—his sin and defeat.

Defending the Glory Today

Only God Himself knows exactly how He views this principle and applies it to a local church of today. While I'm amazed at how long God seems to, at times, tolerate sin, yet I have also seen the progress of churches come to a complete standstill until sin is dealt with. How God can continue to bless *in spite of sin* I am not sure, especially in light of Joshua chapter 7. Perhaps one explanation is that, "Unto whomsoever much is given, of him shall much be required." (Luke 12:48) Joshua's generation had beheld so much in the way of glory, victory, promises, years of teaching and literally hundreds of years of spiritual lineage, that Achan's disobedience was especially inexcusable. Whereas in many of our churches today we have such a large influx of brand-new people coming out of such a dark, blind and spiritually-ignorant world, that God seems willing to show more patience and long-suffering. The Apostle Peter spoke of the "Long-suffering of God" that "waited in the days of Noah." (I Peter 3:20)

But God's long-suffering is never to be mistaken for His doctrine. Patience is wonderful, but it does not change God's truth nor His requirements. Somewhere, sometime, sin *will be* dealt with: either by the individual who has sinned, by those in spiritual authority, or by God Himself. All sin will be judged, either now or later, either by ourselves in heartfelt repentance or by Him in judgment. And however far off it may be, there is a Great White Throne of judgment looming.

Regardless of how it all works, we oft see that unchecked sin will wreak havoc in a church and the plan of God. Achan's sin and Israel's resulting dilemma are written about for our admonition. Judgment is always preceded by a warning from God, and an immediate if not gradual removal of His glory from His people.

Revelation chapters 2 and 3 bear this out. Unless the angels (pastors) of those reprimanded churches did something about the sin and error in their churches, God was going to take drastic steps of judgment, be it the removal of their candlestick, casting them into tribulation or spewing them out of His mouth: God's spirit was not always going to strive with unrepentant saints—or preachers.

Today it is up to you and I to find the mind of God concerning our local assemblies. In our hearts there must be love, awe and desire for the glory and the presence of Almighty God. We will never have righteous success without it.

Every now and then, I come to a place in God where I feel Him nudging and I know it is time. I begin to fast and pray, saying; "I want everything and anything, no matter what it is, that is blocking your glory and revival in this church to be taken out. I want people to be delivered from sin. I want our hearts, spirits and minds to be cleansed, renewed and set free. If anyone clings to sin and refuses to let go, then I guess they will have to be dragged out with it, because I want the sin removed."

Several times through the years I have done this, always with dread in my heart. Because whenever I have sought God like this, it never fails that I will see His power to cleanse His people, and also the power of sin to take people away. I remember one such a season when, in the course of a 4 month period of time, we lost *several* families and individuals. We suffered sorrow and some distress, but in spite of it the glory began to return almost immediately. And over the course of several months, many *more* new people came in.

As we only pass through this life once, we don't have time to play games with God. I want the church I pastor to be what God envisioned from before the foundations of the earth.

Paul's Fight for the Glory

In I Corinthians 5:1-5 Paul dealt with the church in Corinth regarding a member who was committing fornication with his father's wife. No one really knows if it was his natural mother or his stepmother, but it really doesn't matter; it was still vile. Paul told them that this sin was "So wicked that even the heathen don't do it." (Tay) To make matters worse, the church was apparently boasting of their magnanimous nature in allowing this state of affairs to go on.

Paul heard about this un-repented wickedness and wrote to tell the Corinthian saints what they must do. "In the name of our Lord Jesus Christ, when ye are gathered together, and my spirit with the power of our Lord Jesus Christ, to deliver such an one unto Satan, for the destruction of the flesh, that the spirit may be saved in the day of the Lord Jesus."

There are different theories as to how this was carried out and just exactly whose spirit it was that Paul was trying to save—the spirit of the fornicator or the spirit of the church. While I personally lean towards the former view, especially in light of this man's later repentance (II Corinthians 2), I think that both outlooks have merit.

Paul commanded the Corinthian church to remove this man from their midst that the "flesh"—*"what is sensual in him,"* (TCNT)— may be destroyed but his spirit be saved.

"To deliver such an one unto Satan for the destruction of the flesh, that the spirit may be saved in the day of the Lord Jesus." (1 Cor 5:5)

The church had to do something to cause this man to awaken to righteousness and admit that he was living in sin. Thankfully, that is exactly what happened. In the second letter to the Corinthians, the man had found repentance, and Paul now told the church that they; "…ought rather to forgive him, and comfort him, lest perhaps such a one should be swallowed up with overmuch sorrow." (2 Cor 2:7)

Now—after he had repented—was the time to show him love and acceptance. The churches acceptance of him while he was committing the sin had blinded the man to his need for repentance. Furthermore, his was not the only spirit being affected. There was another spirit that needed to be saved and that was the spirit—the glory—of the church.

That God Himself did not take the man in hand and deal with him, once again tells us that He *will not defend His glory*. He leaves that up to us; that is—if we care enough to do it.

When God Defends

In spite of all the examples I have cited to the contrary, I do find occasions and special circumstances when God will indeed—defend His glory. He seems to do it at certain times in order to *declare His feelings and set precedence*. Then—once He has made His expression clear—He will back off and leave it in our hands.

One such occasion was in the early days of the New Testament church, when Ananias and Sapphira sold land and kept back part of the price. Ananias brought a portion of the money as an offering and laid it at the Apostle Peter's feet, while implying that he was giving the entire amount of the sale. Under the unction of the Holy Ghost, Simon said to Ananias, "Why hath Satan filled thine heart to lie to the Holy Ghost, and keep back part of the price of the land? Whiles it remained was it not thine own? And after it was sold was it not in thine own power? Why has thou conceived this thing in thine heart? Thou hast not lied unto men but unto God." (Acts 5:3-4) At these words Ananias fell down dead, slain by God. When his wife came later the same scenario took place, and she was also judged and slain by God. The sin of this couple was *not* in keeping back part of the proceeds, but in lying to God about their generosity. As you can imagine, great fear came upon the churches.

Except for a somewhat obscure but utterly fascinating remark by Paul in I Corinthians 11:30 concerning weak, sickly and sleeping saints who did not bother to discern the sanctity of communion, there is no other record in the New Testament that God ever slew anyone in the church again. But this one occasion does reveal much about His feelings concerning lying and pretension in the things of God.

Personally, I don't think what Ananias and Sapphira did was nearly as repulsive as what the fornicator did in 1st Corinthians 5. Weighed on my scales, I think the incestuous fornicator was far more 'sick' than the hypocritical benefactors. So why didn't God kill the fornicator like He did the deceitful givers? In the same vein, why did God send fire to consume Nadab and Abihu, the sons of Aaron who offered 'strange fire', and yet allow the wicked sons of Eli to steal offerings and commit adultery for years before finally having them slain by uncircumcised Philistines? Why would God kill Er and On, the sons of Judah, for their wickedness, but leave it up to Joshua to slay Achan, the son of Carmi, for his covetousness? Why would God slay Uzzah for simply touching a wobbling Ark, to then allow Israel to completely lose track of it centuries later?

We will never have the answers to all of the questions asked on this side of Heaven. However, we do know that with Ananias, Sapphira, Nadab, Abihu and Uzzah, God was setting precedent. He was establishing His requirement of sincere holiness on the part of His people.

Forgiveness and Restoration

It is equally important to understand that once the Corinthian fornicator repented and came back, he was no longer a fornicator. He repented with godly sorrow and received forgiveness from God. Once that was done, Paul said, 'Accept him and be good to him. Receive him back.' Paul had spurred the Corinthian church to take the necessary steps to help this man find repentance that his spirit could be saved. The church, in doing their painful part, saved not just the man but the Holy Spirit of the assembly as well. Now they were being called upon to restore him.

While saints must be willing to defend the glory, with all that that entails, they should never take on the role of the pastor or become the 'FBI of Pentecost.' Saints must always let the pastor be the pastor. He must be allowed time and space to deal with people and problems. Although at times it may seem like the pastor is not on top of things, or doesn't know what is going on, that still does not give anyone else pastoral authority. He may be dealing with the problems but not announcing that fact to the world. Maybe it has already been dealt with. Maybe he is in the process of feeling out exactly what to do. At any rate, saints should be glad they are not the ones who will have to stand before God in judgment. And when the pastor has issued righteous judgment, the saints should back him to the hilt.

God's Usual Method of Cleansing

The usual procedure that God uses in dealing with sin in the saints begins with trying to reason with their minds and hearts (conscience and emotions). If a person does not listen or repent on their own, then there will come a church service where God will direct that the issue be preached about. Hopefully, at that point the individual will say, "God's been dealing with me about this and now has spoken to me through His word. I am going to do something about it." It is never wise to brush off the preaching of God's word. If it is brushed off, God will then try to reach us in other ways. But note that He most always deals first with kindness, patience and His word. He will then 'move on' to other methods in order to break through the hardening effects of sin. Please take note of the following examples of Jesus' wisdom in dealing with hearts that are less malleable than He desires.

In Mark 6:7 the disciples were commissioned to go out and preach the gospel, cast out devils and heal the sick. *Jesus gave* them the power to do this, and at the same time stripped them of all visible means of support. *He took* their money, bread, purses, extra staves and coats. The Lord gave, but He also took away.

With nothing but God to depend on they went out to preach, and did so with great success. Upon their return they told him, "...all things, both what *they* had done and what *they* had taught" (verse 30). (Note that *they*, the apostles, gave Jesus *not one word* of praise or thanks for the power and success He had given them). As a result of their preaching and miracles the people came "thither afoot out of all cities." Jesus then began to teach their famished hearts. When the day was far spent, His disciples urged Him to send the people away, as they had nothing to eat for their famished stomachs.

Seeing the disciples had not 'gotten the message' of their utter dependency on Him—even though He sent them out to preach penniless—He set about to try their self-sufficiency. He therefore told His disciples, "Give ye them to eat" (vs.37), or in other words, 'Okay big boys, since you have so much ability and power, you feed these 5,000 men, plus women and children.'

When they confessed their insufficiency in having only 200 pennyworth in funds and had only one little boy's lunch, Jesus appropriated the lunch. He blessed it, brake it, and with it—fed the 5,000 men let alone women and children. Still He received no word of thanks or praise from His apostles.

After feeding the thousands and sending them away, He constrained His disciples to get into a boat. (vs.45) They apparently didn't want to go, but they were compelled to get in and cross to the other side of the lake. Meanwhile, Jesus went up to the mountain to pray.

The disciples soon found themselves in a horrific storm. While they strained at the oars, Jesus came by, walking upon the water. Thinking that He was a ghost, they cried out (no doubt to God), and He replied, "Be of good cheer: it is I; be not afraid." (6:50) The wind and waves stopped, calm reigned and the disciples were "...sore amazed in themselves beyond measure, and wondered." (Mark 6:51)

Verse 52 informs us why they were so astonished: "For they considered not the miracle of the loaves; **for their heart was hardened**."

Having a hardened, insensitive heart should be a fate feared by any child of God. Nothing will rob us of blessings more thoroughly than a hardened heart. Nothing will blind us to the beautiful blessings of God more certainly than an insensitive spirit.

It is vital for us to understand that we most desperately need Him. The sensitive and thankful will recognize this through His daily provision for our needs. If we ever begin to think, as the disciples did, that our spiritual and material success is based on something that 'we have done or taught' then we have a lot to learn, and that through possibly painful lessons.

God is faithful, loving and patient and does His best to teach us. He will use the miracle of the breaking of the bread (the preaching of the word), service after service. If we don't get the message that way, He will be forced to use other means. If He must speak three times to Simon Peter through a crowing rooster, He will. If it takes giving the same vision three times to get His message through, He will do that, also. God even has a way of putting us into our own personal boat and bringing us into our own personal storm that we can awaken to our own personal revelation of our need of Him. He simply wants His work to go forward through obedient, sensitive hearts. We may make mistakes and do stupid things, but if we keep a tender heart God will eventually get through to us so we can make things right.

But where there is intransigence and a refusal to repent, there will be great trouble. If there is no surrender to God, it will affect what and how God performs in the individuals life. This is equally true in a church body. The more tender people are—the more quickly they respond and come boldly to the throne of grace—the more His glory can and will fall.

Moses' Standard of Sanctifying

A few years ago I was able to spend every Tuesday morning for three years visiting with a very learned Rabbi from Santa Maria,

California (I have yet to meet an un-learned Rabbi). On one occasion I asked him about Exodus 19:15-16 concerning the sanctification of the people. I asked him about the injunction of Moses that the men come not at their wives. Why did Moses command for the men to "Come not at your wives." And what did Moses base this action upon? Was it Rabbinical opinion that God directed Moses to do this?

"And he said unto the people, Be ready against the third day; come not at your wives. And it came to pass on the third day in the morning, that there were thunders and lightnings, and a thick cloud upon the mount, and the voice of the trumpet exceeding loud; so that all the people that was in the camp trembled."

Rabbi Raich, who is very well-versed in the Old Testament and Jewish tradition, answered that in all the studies he'd ever made, he could find no precedent whatsoever for Moses' decree. It is commonly believed to be strictly an edict of Moses, issued because he alone thought it was a good idea. However, this injunction became a general principle for Israel during special times of sanctification. The Apostle Paul may have drawn from this Mosaic precept of abstinence when mentioning prayer and fasting in 1 Corinthians 7:5.

One could easily say that if God didn't give Moses that decree, he should not have instituted it. My question is, once Moses said it, did God honor it or not? Obviously the answer is yes. God did honor it, just as He honored other decrees Moses gave, such as the one concerning divorce (see Deuteronomy 24:1 and Matthew 19:7-8). Whatever Moses taught—Israel was expected to obey.

The First 'Standard' in the Bible

"Now the serpent was more subtil than any beast of the field which the Lord God had made. And he said unto the woman, Yea, hath God said, Ye shall not eat of every tree of the garden?" (Genesis 3:1).

What the devil is basically asking Eve is, 'Did God *really* say that you could not eat it?' She answers, "We may eat of the fruit of the trees of the garden, but of the fruit of the tree that is in the midst of the garden, God hath said, ye shall not eat of it, neither shall ye touch it lest ye die" (Verses 2 and 3).

There is no record that Eve ever heard God give the commandment concerning this tree and its fruit. God gave Adam the commandment (Genesis 2:17) *before* Eve was created. What He had specifically said to Adam was, "But of the tree of the knowledge of good and evil, thou shalt not eat of it: for in the day that thou eatest thereof thou shalt surely die." God never said anything about 'not touching it.' Technically speaking, Eve *could* have touched, yea she could have juggled the fruit. She could have taken it home and placed it on her kitchen table. What she could *not* do was eat of it, because God said, 'Don't eat it lest ye die.' The specific injunction against the touching of the fruit *could only* have come from Adam.

In my mind, I picture Adam walking with his newly-created wife through the garden, telling her the names of all the animals and plants. As he approaches to the tree of the knowledge of good and evil he says, 'Eve, we can eat of all the fruit of the garden except this fruit. This is the tree of the knowledge of good and evil. We can't even touch this fruit because the day we do, we are going to die!'

In his 'un-fallen' pure love for her he made an effort to protect her from death. He warned his wife not to eat—not to even touch this fruit. Later, as Eve walked about the garden, the devil, through the body of the serpent, came to her and played upon her lack of direct communication with God in this matter. His ploy was to place a dangerous question in her mind, 'Did your husband Adam really hear from God?'

Her answer reveals the very first 'standard' in the Bible; 'do not touch.' This 'standard' was introduced by the first man, in the first home, in an effort to prevent the first and most far reaching fall. Had Eve kept Adam's standard—of not even touching the fruit—she obviously could have never eaten it. Once the fruit was touched it was just a matter of time (literally seconds) before she ate it. Adam's rule was a fence placed a few feet from the precipice to keep her from falling into the canyon below. I would like to compare Adam to a pastor, doing what he could to shield her from destruction.

One might say, "Adam lied and added to the word of God." But how could he lie when he had not yet fallen? He was still pure and innocent. All he knew was the love and commandment of God. Because he was yet in the image of God he could only speak love and truth. Again, one could say, "Adam just wanted to show who was boss and make a bunch of rules and regulations." No, he loved his bride and did not want her to be destroyed. Time proved him to be correct for—once she touched—she did indeed eat. As for Adam, he started down the slippery slope when he allowed his affection for Eve to compel him to break his own rule, and then God's law.

As a minister in this 21st century I think it would have been wonderful to have been the pastor of the Garden of Eden. All he would have to do was get up and say, "Don't anybody touch or eat the fruit of the tree of the knowledge of good and evil. God bless you, I'll see you next week." That would have been it. Alas, our lives have been immeasurably complicated by this modern inventive society. "Lo, this only have I found, that God made man upright; but they have sought out many inventions." (Ecclesiastes 7:29) Thankfully, however complicated life may be, God's lines and precepts never change and are still applicable. He "...hath given us **all things that pertain unto life and godliness,** through the knowledge of Him who hath called us to **glory and virtue.**" (II Peter 1:3)

The first standard in the Bible was given on the basis of love. There was within this standard both line and precept. The line (commandment) was "don't eat of the fruit," the precept (principle) was "don't even touch it." With Israel's 'pastor,' Moses, the line was "sanctify the people," and the precept was "do not come at your wives for three days."

Commandments and Principles

God gave His lines and precepts through Moses[1], and it is amazing how far He was willing to work with and through Moses in this arrangement. This commitment by God to work 'hand in hand' with God-ordained ministries and their judgment is tremendously important. The concept of God working with His man to teach the people is an integral theme of the Bible.

In Mark 10:2 is says, "...the Pharisees came to him, and asked him, Is it lawful for a man to put away his wife? tempting him. And he answered and said unto them, What did Moses command you?"

It is intriguing that Jesus answered in this manner. He could have replied, "What does the law say?" Instead, he said, "What did **Moses command** you?" Verses 4 and 5 continue, "And they said, Moses suffered to write a bill of divorcement, and to put her away. And Jesus answered and said unto them, For the hardness of your heart **he wrote** you this **precept**."

Note that it does not say "commandment," but rather "precept," and that it was given by Moses because of the hardness of their hearts. Did God honor the precept that Moses gave? Without question, just as He still honored the seat of authority that Moses once held. Matthew 23:1 states, "Then spake Jesus to the multitude and to his disciples, saying, The **scribes and the Pharisees sit in Moses' seat**: **All** therefore whatsoever they bid you observe, **that observe and do**."

It is easy to picture someone saying, 'But Jesus, the scribes and Pharisees are a bunch of hypocrites. You yourself pronounced woe upon them. Why should we do what they say?' The answer Jesus gives is, 'Do *what* they say,' but he goes on to say in verse 3, "But do **not** ye **after their works**; for they say and do not." Jesus admonished the people to do what the Pharisees and Sadducees *said*, because of their place of authority, but *not to live like them* because they were hypocrites and "whited sepulchres full of dead men's' bones."

He further said of the Pharisees that, "They bind heavy burdens and grievous to be born, and lay them upon men's shoulders; but they themselves will not lift them with one of their fingers" (verse 4). Jesus dealt with these leaders after their folly and carnality. He is also letting us know that being in a place of authority is never a ticket to run roughshod over God's people, or to lord over them according to our whims or profit. Paul and Peter both dealt with this attitude. "Not that we have dominion over your faith, but are helpers of your joy...." (II Corinthians 1:24) "Neither as being lords over God's heritage, but being ensamples to the flock." (I Peter 5:3) What is best for God's people will always be kept first in the heart and mind of a true shepherd.

The Word of God, the Spirit of God and the Man of God

How are these lines and precepts to be incorporated into our daily walk with God in this 21st century? God mainly uses three channels for the instruction and perfection of His people: the Word of God, the Spirit of God and the Man (or Men) of God. He used these three avenues consistently in both the Old and New Testaments.

We see this clearly in the New Testament in the 15th chapter of the Acts of the Apostles. Certain men of the Jerusalem church came down to the church of Antioch and taught that, in order for Gentiles to be saved, they had to be circumcised. Paul, the apostle to the Gentiles, knew that the essential circumcision was not that which is done by man, but that which is the "circumcision of Christ...buried with him in baptism." (Colossians 2:12) God had revealed to Paul that baptism in Jesus' name is the equivalent of Old Testament circumcision. Because he understood this, he would not put up with these Judaisers "...no, not for an hour..." (Gal 2:5) but went to Jerusalem to settle the matter.

At the Jerusalem council there was great debate among the apostles and elders. Peter spoke at length, using scripture and his own experiences to show that circumcision after the manner of Moses should not be mandatory for the Gentiles. Paul then set forth his teachings and works that had been wrought among the Gentiles. The final and definitive statement came from James. The essence of his judgment was "...My sentence is that we trouble not them, which from among the Gentiles are turned to God...." (Acts 15:9)

Letters were agreed upon and written, stating that the Gentiles did not have to be circumcised. Paul, Judas and Silas returned to Antioch and read the decrees, which stated that, "It seemed good **to us and to the Holy Ghost** to lay upon you no greater burden...." to the great joy and may I say, relief of the Gentile believers. (Acts 15 :28)

It is important that we understand that three main sources were drawn upon to reach the conclusion of this matter: the **Word** of God, the **Spirit** of God and the **Man** (or Men) of God. This is still God's method today, and our acceptance or rejection of this principle reveals more about ourselves than about anything else. The precedent for New Testament lifestyles in the 21st century can be found in the answers to these questions:

1. What does the scripture say?
2. Does it feel right to 'us,' that is, the apostolic ministry?
3. How does the Spirit of God feel about it; is it gladdened or grieved?

A Man to Follow

Romans 3:1-2 says, "What advantage then hath the Jew? Or what profit is there of circumcision? Much every way: chiefly, because that unto them were committed the oracles of God."

Because they were His people, God intended to bless Israel greatly and in every way. Their greatest blessing was in receiving the laws, teachings, statutes, commandments, judgments and oracles of Almighty God. In the last book of the Law, Deuteronomy, Moses speaks to these chosen, blessed people. Note again the intrinsic role that Moses played in God's process of giving Israel His oracles.

"Now therefore hearken, O Israel, unto the statutes and unto the judgments, **which I teach you**, for to do them, that ye may live, and go in and possess the land which the Lord God of your fathers giveth you. Ye shall not add unto the word which I command you, neither shall ye diminish ought from it, that ye may keep the commandments of the Lord your God which I command you. (Deuteronomy 4:1)

"Behold, **I have taught you statutes and judgments, even as the Lord my God commanded me,** that ye should do so in the land whither ye go to possess it. Keep therefore and do them; for this is your wisdom and your understanding in the sight of the nations, which shall hear all these statutes, and say, Surely this great nation is a wise and understanding people. For what nation is there so great, who hath God so nigh unto them, as the Lord our God is in all things that we call upon him for? And what nation is there so great, that hath statutes and judgments so righteous as all this law, which **I set before you this day?** Only take heed to thyself, and keep thy soul diligently, lest thou forget the things which thine eyes have seen, and lest they depart from thy heart all the days of thy life: but teach them thy sons, and thy sons sons" (verses 5-9).

We know that God's law was Israel's preeminent and eternal blessing. We also know that *God used one man, Moses*, to lead His people out of Egypt and teach them these lines and precepts.

What was the key to Moses' character that made him such a safe man to follow? What was it about him that caused God to trust him, entwine Himself with him and honor what Moses said and did? The answer is found in Numbers 12:3—"Now the man Moses was very meek, above all the men which were upon the face of the earth."

It is a frightening and spiritually dangerous thing to follow a proud person. Proud people eventually—*always* cause problems. The higher they are in leadership roles, the more dangerous they are and the more problems they create. But the man Moses, being meek, loved the people of God and labored always for *their* benefit.

When Israel worshipped the golden calf, they so angered God that He said to Moses, "Now therefore let me alone, that my wrath may wax hot against them, and that I may consume them; and I will make thee a great nation...." (Exodus 32:10) An egotistical man would have jumped at the chance of becoming the "new Abraham." Moses, however, "Besought the Lord his God and said, Lord why doth thy wrath wax hot against thy people...Turn from thy fierce wrath, and repent of this evil against thy people. Remember Abraham...." (vs.11-12) God was entreated of Moses and thus spared Israel. God walked with Moses. God used him. God hearkened to him. He was God's mouthpiece to that generation, and an example to every generation since. Like Adam in the garden—and hopefully—the ministry today, Moses' only thought was to protect those whom God had called him to lead and love.

A man like that can be followed safely.

(Footnotes)

[1] *After the first Ten Commandments God continued giving commandments through Moses, until there were altogether 613. It is interesting to note that 365 of them are negative in nature: "thou shalt not." 248 are of a positive nature: "thou shalt." The Hebrews of old believed that there were 248 bones in the human body. (Although there isn't, it was a pretty good guess). Their philosophy was that, as there were 248 positive commandments, for every bone in your body there was something you should do. As there were 365 days in a year, for every day of the year there was something you should not do.*

Chapter Four

The Indispensable Ordinances

The commandments of God are important to Him and He expects them to be important to us. Just how important is seen in Isaiah 58:1-3: (Note; I am purposely leaving out a portion of the text) "Cry aloud, spare not, lift up thy voice like a trumpet, and shew my people their transgression, and the house of Jacob their sins. Yet they seek me daily, and delight to know my ways...they ask of me the ordinances of justice; they take delight in approaching to God. Wherefore have we fasted...."

This text is speaking of a religious body of people who seek God daily; that is, they pray *every day*. They delight to know His ways and they ask of God "the ordinances of justice." They take delight in approaching God; that is, they enjoy praising Him. And they are a people who actually *fast*. At face value they sound like a good, dedicated group of believers. God, however, sees the bigger picture, and to Him something is entirely amiss: "Cry aloud, spare not, lift up thy voice like a trumpet, and shew my people their **transgression,** and the house of Jacob their **sins.**"

Let's consider what they were *not* doing. Verse 2 says that they did all of these things, "as a nation **that did righteousness, and forsook not the ordinance** of their God" (this is the part purposely omitted above). These people did everything *but keep the commandments of God,* which is always 'bad business.'

It is important to understand what God is saying here. He does not care how much you pray, how often you fast, how fervently you worship, or what you know about justice; **if you do not keep His commandments** your sins and transgressions will be declared "like a trumpet." Anyone who can disobey God's word with impunity, regardless of religious gestures, is headed for destruction. "Whoso despiseth the word shall be destroyed...." (Proverbs 13:13)

Furthermore, God will treat us with the same respect that we show His word. "Thus saith the Lord, The heaven is my throne and the earth is my footstool; where is the house that ye build unto me: and where is the place of my rest? For all those things hath mine hand made, and all those things have been, saith the Lord: **but, to this man will I look,** even to him that is poor and of a contrite spirit, and **trembleth at my word**" (Isaiah 66:1-2). God pays attention to, and finds rest in, the man who keeps His ordinances, and who "trembles" (stands in awe) at His word.

On the other hand, when an individual has no compunction about ignoring God's word, yet continues in a 'form of godliness,' he fulfills verses 3 and 4: "He that killeth an ox is **as if** he slew a man: he that sacrificeth a lamb, **as if** he cut off a dog's neck; he that offereth an oblation, **as if** he offered swine's blood; he that burneth incense, **as if** he blessed an idol. Yea, they have chosen their own ways, and their soul delighteth in their abominations. **I also will choose their delusions** and bring their fears upon them...."

No one can afford to play games with God and His word, as no soul can afford delusion and torment.

In I Corinthians 11:1-2 the Apostle Paul writes: "Be ye followers of me, even as I also am of Christ. Now I praise you, brethren, that ye remember me in all things, and keep the ordinances, as I delivered them unto you." While we are not sure what ordinances Paul had already delivered to the Corinthians and was making reference to, the ordinances that he proceeds to talk about are the ones concerning men *not* having long hair and women *having* long (or, uncut) hair.

There are many churches today, even in Apostolic circles, that refuse to acknowledge this, as well as other ordinances. This is a great mistake that brings tragic consequences. Prayer without obedience does not please God. As far as God is concerned, anyone who gets out of the 'obedience business' might as well quit the 'praying business,' also. "He that turneth away his ear from hearing the law, even his prayer shall be abomination." (Proverbs 28:9) Don't pray if you're not willing to obey. The only prayer that God is concerned with after disobedience to Him has occurred is a heartfelt prayer of repentance. Disobedient, unrepentant people, no matter how much they may pray, praise or learn, are serving only a 'calf of gold.' Serving a god of that nature may be a convenient thing for the carnal mind, but it's of no use when you need a God of grace, glory and deliverance.

Mankind needs a God who can direct his steps, because, quite frankly, we don't know how to do it. "O Lord, I know that the way of man is not in himself: it is not in man that walketh to direct his steps." (Jeremiah 10:23) Left to ourselves, we don't have enough sense to 'come in out of the rain' let alone make it to heaven. Our entire existence was spent in darkness until the Lord shined His light on our path through His word. And we "...do well that ye take heed, as unto a light that shineth in a dark place...." (II Peter 1:19)

A golden calf has no power to lead, give light or anything else. It is God and His word that bring us the true light. He is the one who created us and know what makes us 'tick.' If we will walk with Him and obey His word, the Living God will see us through this dark world to everlasting life. It doesn't have to be confusing or hard to live for God, for "...the way of the righteous is made plain" (Proverbs 15:19).

Issues of Life and Death?

Sometimes when teaching the ordinances of God the question is asked, "Is this really necessary? Are these heaven-or-hell issues?"

Let me begin to answer that by posing another question: Is it a life-

or-death issue for a parent to allow a small child to play in the street? The answer depends on what is coming down the road. If the road is never traveled, and nothing is coming down it, then it wouldn't matter if the child played in the street. But if cars, trucks and semi's travel that road, then, obviously, it is a life-and-death decision.

The child may play out there for years and never get hurt. He or she may pay close attention, have good hearing and be adept in getting out of the way of oncoming vehicles. But if that child is ever run over, none of that will matter. What rationale could a parent find to console them for their poor judgment?

As a pastor, I will stand before God for the decisions I make and the things I teach concerning every soul He places under my care. For a preacher to spiritually say, "It doesn't matter. If you want to play those games in the street, go right ahead," is gross negligence on his part. God help the people who are under the type of pastor who would be willing to 'toss the dice and take a gamble' with the well-being of their souls. God have mercy on the people who trust the judgment of a pastor who doesn't care.

It has been said, "Some preachers make such a big deal out of things that God gave so little space to in scripture!" I believe that Jesus addressed this line of thinking very thoroughly in Matthew 5:18-19: "For verily I say unto you, till heaven and earth pass, one **jot** or one **tittle** shall in no wise pass from the law, till all be fulfilled. Whosoever therefore shall break **one of these least commandments**, and **shall teach men so**, shall be called least in the kingdom of heaven: but whosoever shall **do** and **teach** them, shall be called great in the kingdom of heaven." Some other translations of this text are also informative:

"Whoever therefore tries to **weaken** even **one of these smallest** commandments...." (Lam)

"...disregards the **least significant** of these commandments...." (Ber)

"...a **single one** of these commands, were it **even one of the least**...." (Mof)

"Therefore the man who abolishes **one of these little rules**....." (Rieu)

Jesus is obviously very interested in us keeping even these "least commandments."

One of the greatest compliments I have ever received was not given for any message that I preached, or deed that I did. It came from a man we had won to the Lord years ago. He came to me with tears in his eyes, holding his two beautiful little girls, and said, "Pastor, I want to thank you for making this church a safe place for me to raise my family." This man and his wife were thankful for a pastor who did not let them play in the street. They knew, as well as I, that their "adversary the devil, as a roaring lion, walketh about, seeking whom he may devour...." (I Peter 5:8) In our world there is a pathological killer on the prowl. He is behind the wheel of a vehicle devised for death, stalking the highways and byways, looking for 'children' who are playing outside the boundaries of holiness.

Who Will Shut the Doors?

In the book of Malachi the Lord speaks to His people in a series of statements, questions and answers designed to provoke thoughts that might save them. He begins with the statement "I have loved you saith the Lord." He then asks the question (as coming from Israel) "Yet you say, Wherein hast thou loved us?" He answers, "Was not Esau Jacob's brother...Yet I loved Jacob and I hated Esau...." (chapter 1:2-3)

In chapter 1, verses 6-8 we read: "A son honoureth his father, and a servant his master: if then I be a father, where is my honor? And if I be a master, where is my fear? Saith the Lord of Hosts unto you O priest that despise my name."

Israel replies, "Wherein have we despised thy name?"

God answers, "Ye offer polluted bread upon mine altar."

Israel asks, "Wherein have we polluted thee?"

God answers, "In that ye say the table of the Lord is contemptible. And ye offer the blind for sacrifice...and ye offer the lame and the sick...is it not evil? ...**offer it now unto thy governor;** will he be pleased with thee or accept thy person?"

In verse 12 God indicts them for profaning His name in saying, "The table of the Lord is polluted; and the fruit thereof, even his meat is contemptible," also "What a weariness is it!"

In chapter 3 verse 8 God asks a seemingly ridiculous question: "Will a man rob God?" When they replied, "Wherein have we robbed thee?" God answered, "You have robbed me in tithes and offerings. Ye are cursed with a curse: for ye have robbed me, even this whole nation."

It is obvious that we are dealing with a 'religious' but backslidden people. This last Israelite generation to receive the writings we call the Old Testament were like so many others, in that they "...draw near me with their mouth, and with their lips do honour me, but have removed their heart far from me...." (Isaiah 29:13) We see how much their cold carnality vexed God in Malachi 1:10. In the midst of this discourse, God asks one of the most pointed questions of all—"Who is there even among you that would shut the doors for naught?" God actually became so frustrated with Israel's half-hearted worship and service that He said, 'I wish there was a priest among you who would shut the doors.' Or, to apply it to a New Testament ecclesia, 'I wish that church would just shut down and not even call itself a church.'

A similar case in our own dispensation is seen in the Apostle Paul's letter to the Corinthian church. Because of their lack of reverence concerning the Lord's supper, he said that their coming together was "...not for the better but for the worse." (I Corinthians 11:17) As far as God is concerned, church service that is not carried out in decency and sincerity is worse than no service at all.

That God would actually shut down a church is seen in the book of Revelation. To the once-great church of Ephesus He wrote, "Remember therefore from whence thou art fallen, and repent, and do thy first works; **or else I will come unto thee quickly, and will remove the candlestick** out of his place, except thou repent" (Revelation 2:5). This is not to say that the Ephesians could not continue in their loveless service—any less than Israel in Malachi's day continued in their half-hearted worship. But it did mean that as far as God's presence and glory was concerned—the candlestick was about to be removed.

Hell's Theme Song

If there were a theme song in hell, it would go something like this: "What does it matter, what does it matter? What difference does it make, what difference does it make?" While the world, the devil, backslidden preachers and indifferent saints all claim that holiness unto God and separation from the world no longer matters, "Jesus Christ [is still] the same yesterday, to day, and for ever." (Hebrews 13:8) Scriptural mores have not and never will change. They do make a difference. "Heaven and earth shall pass away, but my words shall not pass away." (Matthew 24:35) Lines still make a difference.

In Luke 16 we read of a beggar named Lazarus and a certain rich man who fared sumptuously every day. The rich man was exceedingly comfortable, but he was lost. The beggar Lazarus was poor, sick and miserable, but he was saved. Outside of these differences all that was between these two men was a gate where Lazarus had been laid. The rich man could have—and after a fashion—did, sing, "What does it matter, what difference does it make?"

After Lazarus and the rich man both died we see the difference. The rich man once more sees Lazarus. Now however, he's not on the other side of a gate, but on the other side of a great, fixed gulf, in Abraham's comforting bosom while he himself is in hell, forever. The rich man found out far, far too late—*what a difference a line can make.*

Abner and the Line

In II Samuel chapter 3 Abner, the captain of the host for Israel's army, found out how important a line can be. After conferring with King David he left the city of Hebron only to be called back by Joab, David's highest general. Having slain Joab's younger brother in a foolish battle, Abner should have known the great peril he was in due to Joab's lust for vengeance. But, back to Hebron he went.

The city of Hebron was one of the six cities of refuge designated by Moses in Numbers chapter 35. A city of refuge was a place where one could find asylum from the "avenger of blood." In those days if a man slew another, whether by accident or design, he was 'free game' to be slain by a kinsman or friend. The only chance to escape such vengeance was to flee to one of the refuge cities. There a trial would be held to determine the man's innocence or guilt. Until this could all take place the only place of protection was within the walls of the city designated for refuge.

The blood of Joab's brother Asahel could not be avenged within the walls of Hebron, as there had been no trial. Furthermore, the case against Abner was weak, since he really didn't mean to kill Asahel, but only to stop his pursuit after the battle. [see II Samuel 2:18-30] Therefore, Joab had to get Abner outside of the city and away from the haven of safety. Once there, Joab could kill Abner with impunity.

They strolled toward the gates of the city arm-in-arm, in what seemed an aimless and harmless excursion. But as soon as they stepped through the gate, Joab pulled a knife free and thrust it under Abner's fifth rib and coldly watched him die. Had Joab committed this act of vengeance on the wrong side of the line, he could have died for it. But because he slyly moved Abner away from the perimeter of safety he could kill without fear of reprisal and apparently without remorse.

One can only speculate what Abner's last thoughts were. They could well have been, 'I have played the fool. If I'd only stayed on the right side of the line I could have lived.' What a difference a boundary can make. What a difference a commandment can make. *What a difference a line can make.*

Samson and the Line

At the direction of the angel of the Lord, Samson's parents placed the Nazarite vow upon him at his birth. This vow required that he never cut his hair, touch the dead body of a man or beast, or eat or drink anything from the fruit of the vine. (Numbers 6:1-10) As long as Samson lived within the confines of the vow placed on him, the spirit of the Lord would come upon him and he would have incredible strength. From the ripping apart of a lion to the slaying of 1,000 men with only the jawbone of an ass, Samson's strength knew no bounds. Alas, Samson's spirit knew no bounds either, and that became his downfall.

On several occasions we find that Samson was a man totally governed by his passions. Nevertheless, as long as he kept at least the portion of the vow that had to do with his hair, God's Spirit, no doubt for His own purposes, would fall upon Samson and give him great strength. [read Judges 13 through 16]

It was not until he finally crossed the line and told Delilah the source of his great strength that his locks were shorn. He then lost his strength and became like any other man. The Philistines came upon him, bound him, and destroyed his eyes. He became a source of mockery for the Philistines and a byword in Israeli history.

What difference did his consecration make? While he kept it, he could destroy lions, carry away massive city gates weighing literally tons, snap off ropes and destroy armies single-handedly. Once the locks of consecration were cut, he became like other men, with a host of enemies and no God to help him. He learned too late *what a difference a line can make.*

Chapter Five

The Fence That Won the West

A few years ago my family and I went to Washington, DC. Of the many famous sights we visited, we found the National Archives building to be one of the most interesting. It was there that we saw the Declaration of Independence, the United States Constitution, the Bill of Rights and the Magna Carta. As I approached the Declaration of Independence, I glanced to my left and something riveted my attention. It was the original patent received by a man named Joseph Glidden, dated November 24, 1874. It was the patent for his famous and widely accepted—barbed wire.

I was captivated by the display as the Smithsonian Institute had just published a list of the top ten inventions (or discoveries) that, in their opinion, had most affected mankind in the last millennium. They were: the printing press, the steam engine, the internal combustion engine, the harnessing of electricity, the telephone, the computer, penicillin, atomic power, television (sad but true) and—believe it or not—barbed wire.

To understand the unbelievable importance of the barbed wire fence, we need to view the world into which it first came. After the Civil War, cattle became a huge industry in the United States due mainly to the westward expansion of the population and the need of the US Army to protect them. The Civil War left a lot of disillusioned people with shattered homes and lives. Many of these people, as well as immigrants, traveled west to find a new life. These migrants had to be protected from Indian tribes who were not exactly keen about having their world torn away from them. The troops protecting these sojourners had to be fed, as well as those who settled in the various areas. Add to this scenario an expanding economy in the well-settled east with a growing desire for beef, and you have an exploding cattle industry.

There were two basic types of people in the American west in those days: the cattlemen who *roamed* the land, and those who *settled* it. The term used to identify the cattlemen was "grangers." The people who settled down were called "nesters" because they "built their nests." In this great American drama the cattlemen played an important role in that they contributed to the feeding of the people. However, they built no cities, schools or churches, and had little business other than cattle. While what they did was important, they were not the creators of society. That was left to the "nesters."

From the beginning, the number one problem between nesters and grangers was over fencing. A granger driving a herd of cattle from Texas to Dodge City for shipping didn't want the process to be hung up by fences strung across the range. But a farmer had to have fences. Anyone building a farm or a community simply had to have a fence.

To build a civilization, three primary elements are needed. The first is protection from the elements, be it a house, a barn, etc. Second; protection from man and his untoward nature, hence the establishment of laws, punishments, weapons, etc. Third; protection from animals, that is, wild beasts, other men's beasts and the settlers' own beasts.

A farmer raising pigs has to have a way to keep his pigs out of the cornfield. He can raise both pigs and corn, but not together on the same spot. They have to be kept separate until the farmer can feed a desired amount of corn to the pigs at a time of his choosing. Fencing is absolutely essential to farming, and agriculture is absolutely essential to civilization. Eventually, as the cattle industry became more business-like and stable, they also saw the need for fencing their herds off from others to prevent straying and rustling. Civilization therefore had to have fences.

***

The Midwest and Southwest are not like the eastern or even the far northwestern parts of the United States. In those regions there are a great amount of trees and forests, and thus a vast amount of wood to build the much-needed fencing. In the New England states there were no great forests but there was an ample amount of rock which could be used to build stone fences, many of which are still in use today. In a few states there was enough rainfall that hedges could be grown for fencing, such as is seen in great abundance in Europe.

But the western U.S. doesn't have enough rainfall to make hedges practical. And while stones are obviously to be found there, how could a stone fence be made long enough and strong enough to controls hundreds—if not thousands of cattle? Where would they find the manpower, let alone all of the rocks, to erect and maintain thousands of miles of stone fence?

While there was plenty of wood in other parts of the nation to facilitate the need, it was impractical that all fencing be supplied by the lumber industry. Even treated wood exposed to the elements requires great amounts of upkeep, and this alone made it prohibitive for use, besides the wood fences great initial expense.

Lack of adequate fencing was stymieing the growth of western society. In order for the United States to continue its progress, some solution was desperately needed. To understand just how big this problem was, I quote from the book, *The Wire That Fenced The West:* "Questions pertaining to fencing occupied more space in public print or newspapers than any other issue in America." It is hard for us to imagine anything in the news taking up more time and space than politics, economics, sports or the latest scandals. And yet the issue of fencing was absolutelty that important.

Enter... the Barbed Wire Fence

In an effort to meet this need, many men set forth to produce practical, affordable fencing. In the decade following the Civil War over 800 fence patents were issued. A large number of these patents were given to men who had designed what came to be known as "barbed wire."

While sales of these various, and somewhat odd-looking, fences were taking place around the nation with varying success, none really captured the imagination of the farmers and ranchers in the west where it was so desperately needed. One of the main reasons for this reluctance was lack of confidence on the part of the cattlemen. It seemed unlikely to them that a few thin strands of wire could hold back even one Texas Longhorn, let alone a whole herd. Events finally transpired however that literally changed history. The fence and the salesman who sold it were what brought that change.

The original patent for this fence is the one I saw at the National Archives. Named "The Winner" by its inventor, it has been called "the wire that fenced the west." The reason it vastly outsold its competitors was not that it was any stronger, or had any distinct advantage by way of design. Its success was due entirely to a 22-year-old salesman named John Gates.

***

John Warner Gates was a depressed young man. A salesman for Joseph Glidden, he just could not sell any barbed wire anywhere. Not even in the cattle town of San Antonio, Texas. Cattlemen, farmers and Texas Longhorns were there aplenty, and they all needed suitable, affordable fencing. But the Texans thought that Gates' thin, scrappy wire was a joke when compared to the strength of the Texas Longhorn. John Warner Gates therefore had no takers for his product. As he sat dejectedly in one of San Antonio's many saloons, he was suddenly hit with an idea that he thought might just turn the trick.

Just outside of town he marked off a huge area with fence-posts and strung them with six strands of his barbed wire. He then published a proclamation daring the rural and city people to come and see an amazing feat. On the appointed day ranchers, farmers, grangers, nesters, and almost everybody came to see Gates foolhardy demonstration.

With the fence in place, Gates' hired men began herding hundreds of Texas Longhorns into the enclosed area. The Texans dealt with these creatures on a daily basis and were familiar with both their strength and wild nature. The onlookers laughed, saying, "There is *no way* that fence is going to hold those Longhorns." They plainly thought Gates was crazy.

But as the Longhorns were herded in, the doubters were amazed as they watched them rush up to the fence, brush against it, and then back away from it. They'd 'hit it a lick' and then decide that it wasn't such a good idea to get too close to it. After a while—to everyone's astonishment—the Longhorns settled down.

Then an even more amazing thing happened. Some say John Gates himself did it, others say he hired somebody to do it—but whoever did it must have been desperate for money. Someone took a fire torch and ran into the midst of the Longhorns, swinging it around their head and screaming like a banshee. The cattle, though crazed with fear and running pell-mell within the confines of the fence, *did not tear it down*. At this point John Gates leapt to a platform holding a strand of the barbed wire and bellowed, *"This is the finest fence in the world! It's as light as air, stronger than whiskey and cheaper than dirt!"*

This unique ad campaign caught the imagination of the Texans, and soon the rest of the west. They realized that this fence was what they had been looking for—and the boom was on.

Glidden's company sold 10,000 lbs. of barbed wire in 1874.

The next year it sold 600,000 lbs. of wire.
In 1876 they sold 2,840,000 lbs.,
In 1877 they sold 12,863,000 lbs.,
In 1878 they sold 26,655,000 lbs.,
In 1879 they sold 50,300,000 lbs., and
In 1880 they sold 80,500,000 lbs. of Glidden's wire.

Many other competitors quickly went out of business, but the fence named "The Winner" definitely became the winner. The 22-year-old John Warner Gates became rich and is today credited with being the man who built the city of Port Arthur, Texas.

And this is why barbed wire is considered by the Smithsonian Institute to be one of the top 10 most important inventions of all time. Without it, there could not have been the settling and civilizing of the West.

Fence-posts and Fences—Lines and Precepts

Glidden's fence was not the only barbed wire fence invented. In fact it was but one of literally hundreds, with many of them having much the same ability to perform. For a farmer who used "The Winner" to call his neighbor a fool for using another brand would not have been very wise himself. The man who purchased the brand of fence called "Baker's Perfect" or "Brotherton Bob" to use on his ranch might well say, "It may be a little different from yours… but it works for me." While there were differences as to the fine points of the various fences (excuse the pun) they were all basically similar in design. They all were made of strands of steel, had their variously-shaped and spaced barbs, and were strung on wooden fence-posts. Most importantly, they all could hold back unwanted intruders.

***

In the Oneness Holiness movement there are no two churches just alike though there are, for the most part, many similarities. Sometimes, for the saints, experiencing these differences between the various churches can be somewhat troubling. The main reason for these differences is very simple; *there are no two pastors just alike.* Being humans, they each have their own personalities, points of theological interest, abilities, circumstances, personal experiences, backgrounds and histories. It is not surprising, therefore, that there are differences of opinion as to certain aspects of life in general and church life in particular. Alas—and here we are again—there are many "tribes in Israel."

Over the years I have come to appreciate pastors who are *willing to even put up a fence,* let alone having one that is exactly like mine. Our views of lines and precepts may not agree in every detail, but if they are sincerely trying to keep the world out of the Lord's vineyard, I—and no doubt the Angels—applaud them.

As an example of one of these differences, I know of pastors who feel that a woman's hair should be worn up on her head at all times when in public. While I do not personally hold to this view, I respect it. Whatever one's views on how a woman's hair is to be worn, surely we must agree that it is not to be cut—that is the 'line' in the Word, and it is plain in its declaration. All that I personally ask the ladies that I pastor is that their hair look 'nice,' whether it be worn up or hangs down, and that it be a presentable Christian witness. I usually enjoin this request with the observation that no Christian enjoys having a pastor who is an embarrassment in lifestyle, speech or appearance. The same is true in regards to a pastor and the people he pastors—he does not enjoy being embarrassed by *their* lifestyle, speech or appearance.

I personally do not have the time to answer for everyone else and their standards, or lack thereof. However, I do have a deep sense of responsibility for the people I pastor, and towards the God that I serve. Though not everyone understands or appreciates the teaching and guidelines of a conscientious shepherd, we must nevertheless do our duty and fulfill our call, that of presenting a bride to Jesus Christ. The Apostle Paul said it best: "Would to God ye would bear with me in my folly: and indeed bear with me. For I am jealous over you with a godly jealousy: for I have espoused you to one husband, that I may present you as a chaste virgin to Christ." (II Corinthians 11:1-2)

"Wherefore I take you to record this day, that I am pure from the blood of all men. For I have not **shunned to declare unto you all the counsel of God.** Take heed therefore unto yourselves, and to all the flock, over the which the Holy Ghost hath made you overseers, to feed the church of God, which he hath purchased with his own blood... And now brethren I commend you to God, and to the word of his grace, which is able to build you up, and to give you an inheritance among all them which are sanctified." (Acts 20:26-28, 32)

***

In order for the West to be civilized, it was essential that boundaries be created that cattle, sheep, hogs and men would honor. Likewise in the Kingdom of God, there must be established lines and precepts. It was lines and precepts that separated Israel from all other peoples of the world. It was the keeping of commandments that made them a people blessed and used of God. They inevitably faltered and failed once they forsook the lines and precepts God had given them. We must ever keep in mind the tribe of Israel that received the severest judgment during the wilderness sojourn. Simeon suffered devastating losses because of one single aspect of their character—they were a tribe who had no fences. Nothing was too cruel or profane for them. Lines and precepts concerning sanctity and separation were foreign to them and they suffered accordingly.

The Tragedy of a Fenceless Flock

Years ago I attended a General Conference where a special session, only for ministers was held. A certain pastor had been asked to speak to the ministers about his personal experiences concerning the importance of upholding holiness in the local church. I knew that the church he pastored had about 600 people at the time, and I also knew that they had let down tremendously in separation from the world.

This pastor related to us how that on three separate occasions God dealt with him about His displeasure with this situation of waning holiness. He would not say how God had talked to him the first time, but he did tell how God dealt with him the final two times.

In the first instance, he told of purchasing a piece of property in the country where he had placed some sheep. When he bought the small flock, a few goats were also 'thrown in' by the seller. At the time the pastor thought this was a kind gesture, but he soon realized why the goats were free.

In the middle of his property he fenced off an area and put up a shelter with food and water for his flock. One morning he came to check on them and found they had all broke through the fence and were grazing beyond its perimeters. He found the breach, repaired it and managed to get them all back inside.

The next day the animals were out again: not far away, just a few feet outside the fence. He thought to himself that there must be something there that they wanted and needed, so he enlarged the fences border just enough to include the area where the sheep and goats had been grazing. He said to himself; "Now you will be happy. This is what you wanted!"

When he came back the following day, they were again outside the fence: not far, but just beyond the bounds that he *thought* would make them happy. He repaired the breach and once more herded them all back inside, only to come back another day and find them outside. He enlarged the fence yet once more, saying, "OK, this is where you want to be. The fence is now big enough to accommodate your desire." But the next day they were outside the fence again. Through this process he realized that it was the goats that were the real instigators of these 'breakouts' and understood why they had been given to him for free.

The property where he kept his flock was surrounded on all sides by a fence and dirt roads. The fence surrounding the property obviously had little ability to keep the sheep and goats in, and the pastor was frustrated and tired of the animals constantly getting out. He figured there would be nothing appealing in the road for them to eat, and would therefore probably be safe enough. So he removed the inner fence completely. His attitude was, "All right, go ahead and have the whole field! I'll let them do whatever they want. I know they can get through the main fence but why would they want to? They'll be all right."

Early one morning he received a phone call from a neighboring farmer. He said, "Preacher, you had better come down here. You've really got a mess on your hands. A pack of wild dogs came through last night and they've slaughtered your flock."

When the pastor arrived on the scene he found every sheep and every goat dead. Their stomachs and throats had been ripped out and the carnage was gruesome. The dogs didn't even eat them; they just slew the flock in a blood lust and left them while they yipped and yapped their way back to whatever pit they came from.

As he stood there in the midst of the blood and gore, looking at his slaughtered flock, the Lord God spoke to him these words: ***"Fences are not just to keep things in, they are also to keep some things out."*** The pastor was now thunderstruck as well as sick.

He understood clearly that God was talking to him about placating the carnality in his church by continually letting down on standards of Holiness. In so doing, all he had accomplished was to enlarge the fence time after time, with the flock ever desiring to go beyond it (no doubt being led by "goats"). A worldly spirit had already been loosed in the church and many of the people were murmuring and complaining about what few standards were left. [It would be interesting to know who had loosed that worldly spirit to begin with]

It is important for us to remember that fences keep more things *out* than they keep *in*. Bible-based guidelines for Christian living are not just to keep Christians *in*. This world is full of wild, roving predators that delight in dragging souls to the same hell where they themselves are headed. God bless the pastor who does not weary in well doing, but continues to teach, preach and exemplify Christian values and lifestyle. There are evil spirits, eroding philosophies, specious doctrines, aberrant lifestyles and blatant sins that are all working overtime to worm their way into God's church. Once there, their only intent is to kill, maim and destroy.

The second incident that this pastor related to us took place one day while he was praying in the balcony of his church auditorium. He was extremely frustrated and had stated to God; "I am so tired and weary of fussing with these people. I am not even going to preach holiness anymore." At that moment God spoke to him in an audible voice and said: *"And if you do, I will remove your candlestick. This is the third time that I have spoken to you concerning this matter. I will never speak to you about it again."*

The pastor crumbled, slid out of his seat and literally crawled down the steps of the balcony on his hands and knees to his office. He grabbed a pen from his desk and on a note pad wrote the exact words that God had spoken to him.

The next Sunday morning he preached a message entitled: "Buy the Truth and Sell It Not." In that sermon he let it be known that they, as the people of God, were going back to the Biblical standards of Holiness and separation from the world. That particular Sunday was known thereafter as "Black Sunday." One-third of his church got up and walked out. They left and started another church in town with a "preacher" from within the congregation. The religion they embraced was of the golden calf variety. They could do anything they wanted and still claim a form of godliness.

This pastor stood his ground and within the next couple of weeks, 60 people received the baptism of the Holy Ghost. God poured out His Glory and confirmed to that pastor and congregation that He still wants His people to "Worship Him in the beauty of Holiness." (Psalm 29:2)

While he was relating his story to the conference, an elderly pastor who had been faithful to God through the years leaned over to a friend of mine and said, "I hope he makes it. I really hope he makes it. The problem is, I've been preaching this gospel for over 50 years and I've never seen anybody let holiness go as far as he has and ever really come back."

To the deep grief of my heart, I must report that the elder was right. That pastor with whom God had dealt three times about holiness did not make it. Somewhere along the line he had lost his willingness to "Contend for the faith once delivered unto the Saints." (Jude 3) He ceased to be a pastor several years ago and that church is today unrecognizable in terms of holiness, godliness and New Testament doctrine. God removed the candlestick as He said He would, and also apparently kept His word to never speak to the man again about the doctrine of holiness. Again, to the deep grief of my heart, the last I heard of him he was selling goods on the side of the road.

Dear reader, this is grim, serious business with God if it does not work its way into the depths of our hearts. Separation *from* the ungodliness of this world should come naturally to the child of God as he draws *nigh* unto Him. If holiness unto the Lord is not important, then why did God repeatedly incorporate its precepts and principles into His word? And if a person refuses by obey God in this area, why obey Him in any area?

Through the years I have seen far too many men change and say, "This isn't for me. We don't need that holiness stuff anymore." They proceed in their folly and lead their families and churches astray from the paths of righteousness. I have watched in horror as their children have been spiritually decimated, their families thrown to the winds, and their churches brought to nothing spiritually and, in many cases, literally. In the process of tearing down the fences of a God-ordained life, they fulfill Ecclesiastes 10:8: "...whoso breaketh an hedge, **a serpent shall bite him.**" We can break through and tear down the hedges that God has set, but remember that there is a serpent (the devil) always looking for a breach, that he may enter in to slay God's people. He longs to sink poisonous fangs into anyone who would tear down the fences of safety that God and godly men have constructed.

The Apostle John tells us to, "Love not the world, neither the things that are in the world. If any man love the world, the love of the Father is not in him. For all that is in the world, the lust of the flesh, and the lust of the eyes, and the pride of life, is not of the Father, but is of the world." (I John 2:15,16)

Philippians 4:8 says, "Finally brethren, whatsoever things are *true*, whatsoever things are *honest*, whatsoever things are *pure*, whatsoever things are *lovely*, whatsoever things are of *good report*; if there be any *virtue* and if there be any *praise*, *think on these things*." [emphasis mine]

In the following chapters I will attempt to address several of the most important issues facing the Apostolic Church today, concerning holiness and separation from the world. I will not be able to cover every issue, nor will I be able to cover any of them completely. Are they *all* heaven-or-hell issues? Whether they are or not, if they have the power to beset us or cause us to veer away from God's Grace and Glory, they must be dealt with and settled righteously in our hearts. The writer of Hebrews says it best: "...let us **lay aside every weight and the sin** which doth **so easily beset us**...." (Hebrews 12:1).

Some other translations state the verse on this wise:

"...Stripping off every encumbrance...." (Rhm)

"...Let us fling aside every encumbrance that so readily entangles our feet...." (Wey)

"...Let us throw off every impediment...." (Wms)

"...Let us also lay aside everything that hinders us...." (TCNT)

"...Let us rid ourselves of everything that weights us down...." (Knox)

Woe be to the man who makes light of sacred things. Woe be to the tribe that scoffs at sanctity as did the Simeonites. Woe be to those who "...walk after the flesh, in the lust of uncleanness, and despise government. Presumptuous are they, self-willed, they are not afraid to speak evil of dignities...." (II Peter 2:10)

Some other translations II Peter 2:10:

"...Who yield to their physical nature and indulge their passions that defile them and despise authority...they stand in no awe of Majesty...." (Gspd)

"...Daring, presumptuous creatures, they think nothing of scoffing at...." (Phi)

"...Audacious and self-willed...." (TCNT)

"...They tremble not to rail at dignities...." (ASV)

"...They do not tremble when they abuse...." (Wms)

The One who created us knows exactly what He wants and what we need. It is a safe, Holy pathway that He has revealed. And He declared it to us because He loves and cares about us.

Chapter Six

Jewelry

66"**W**herefore gird up the loins of your mind, be sober, and hope to the end for the grace that is to be brought unto you at the revelation of Jesus Christ; As obedient children, not fashioning yourselves according to the former lusts in your ignorance: But as he which hath called you is holy, so **be ye holy in all manner of conversation** [lifestyle]; Because it is written, Be ye holy; for I am holy" (I Peter 1:13-16).

As children of God, what about us should be holy?
  Our bodies should be holy (Romans 12:1)
  Our hair should be holy (I Corinthians 11:7)
  Our eyes should be holy (Job 31:1)
  Our mouth should be holy (Matthew 12:37)
  Our lips should be holy (Hosea 14:2)
  Our tongues should be holy (Acts 2:11)
  Our speech should be holy (Colossians 4:6)
  Our hands should be holy (I Timothy 2:8)
  Our hearts should be holy (Romans 5:5)
  Our minds should be holy (Hebrews 10:16)
  Our thoughts should be holy (Psalm 139:23-24)
  Our feet should be holy (Hebrews 12:13)
  Our dress should be holy (I Timothy 2:9)
  Our deeds should be holy (Romans 2:6)
  Our spirit should be holy (I Corinthians 6:20)
  Our time should be holy (Ephesians 5:16)
  Our worship should be holy (I Chronicles 16:29)
  Our faith should be most holy (Jude 20)

There is no pertinent facet of life that is not given full coverage in the word of God.

"According as his divine power hath **given unto us all things that pertain unto life and godliness**, through the knowledge of him that hath **called us to glory and virtue.**" (II Peter 1:3)

As children of God we are not only to "...abhor that which is evil; cleave to that which is good," (Romans 12:9), but we are to "Abstain from all **appearance** of evil." (I Thessalonians 5:22) As we do this is it allows "...the very God of peace [to] sanctify you wholly," and makes way for our "...whole spirit and soul and body [to] be preserved blameless unto the coming of our Lord Jesus Christ." (I Thessalonians 5:22,23)

***

This chapter concerns jewelry and what the word of God has to say about it. The question is; should Christians wear it? As an answer, it is simply not enough to say, "Jewelry is wrong, therefore do not wear it." Scriptural answers, insights and reasons must be brought forth as to why it is not pleasing to God. This generation demands it, and God does not mind giving it. This discussion therefore is a heartfelt attempt to shed light upon a subject that has suffered from much misinformation if not good intentions.

The Importance of Understanding

I Peter 3:15 tells us to "...sanctify the Lord God in your hearts: and be ready always to give an answer to every man that asketh you a reason...." When honest-hearted people receive understanding about the whys and wherefores of Bible commandments, it makes obedience easier. Parents often ask their children to do things that they may not comprehend, such as, "Don't play in the street." Hopefully they obey in spite of their lack of understanding of the dangers. As they grow older—or they almost get run over— understanding makes it easier for them to obey. We try to teach our children the difference between what is, right and wrong—good and bad—acceptable and unacceptable—proper and improper—safe and unsafe—so that they can be successful saints and citizens. We also do it to protect them from as many harmful things in life as possible. So it is with our God. Obedience to His word, whether we understand it all or not, is our very greatest protection.

Things Once Allowed...But No More

Prior to, and even during, the dispensation of Mosaic Law, God allowed things in the lives of His people that He does not allow in the New Testament dispensation of grace. In several regards, the New Testament is stricter and more binding than the Old Testament. The following are a few examples of things that were allowed then but are not acceptable now: divorce for any cause—polygamy, or having more than one wife—the taking of human life in personal vengeance or battle—and the wearing of jewelry.

Divorce... for any cause

If a man wished to divorce his wife under Mosaic Law, he simply wrote out words to that effect and handed her the "bill of divorcement." At that point, both he and she were free to remarry someone else. (Deuteronomy 24: 1-3) But now, the Lord has commanded that divorce and remarriage is allowable only in cases where one of the parties has engaged in illicit sex. "And I say unto you, Whosoever shall put away his wife, except it be for fornication, and shall marry another, committeth adultery: and whoso marrieth her which is put away doth commit adultery" (Matthew 19:9). God *now* requires more.

Polygamy

In the Old Testament men were allowed to have more than one wife. Although this was a common practice, especially among the kings, there was not one case where it didn't cause deep and manifold problems within the family (consider the immediate families of Abra-

---

ham, Jacob and David). There was no restriction on the number of wives a man might have except for the king of Israel, whose lifestyle and leadership set the tone for the entire nation. But even then, the only restriction stated was that he not "multiply wives unto himself" (Deuteronomy 17:17). While no one really knew exactly what that nebulous number might be, Talmudic teaching is that anything over *seventeen* was too many. However, the New Testament requires that leaders be "...the husband of *one* wife...." (I Timothy 3:2). This is vastly different than what was required under the dispensation of Law. Grace *now* requires more.

The Taking of Human Life

In the Old Testament the taking of human life in time of war or as familial vengeance for a kinsman's life taken by another was permissible. (Deuteronomy 19:4-13, Joshua 20:1-6) King David is an example of an Old Testament saint who engaged in much warfare, yet was called a 'man after God's own heart.' The only place where he was caught-up-short because of it, was when Nathan the prophet told him that he could not build the temple because he had "shed much blood." (II Chronicles 22:8)

Jesus, on the other hand, taught and lived a life of pacification. Isaiah 53:7 tells us, "He was oppressed, and he was afflicted, yet he opened not his mouth: he is brought as a lamb to the slaughter, and as a sheep before her shearers is dumb, so he openeth not his mouth."

And in Matthew 5:38-48 He taught, "Ye have heard that it hath been said, An eye for an eye, and a tooth for a tooth: But I say unto you, That ye resist not evil: but whosoever shall smite thee on thy right cheek, turn to him the other also. And if any man will sue thee at the law, and take away thy coat, let him have thy cloke also. And whosoever shall compel thee to go a mile, go with him twain...Ye have heard that it hath been said, Thou shalt love thy neighbour, and hate thine enemy. But I say unto you, Love your enemies, bless them that curse you, do good to them that hate you, and pray for them which despitefully use you, and persecute you; That ye may be the children of your Father which is in heaven...Be ye therefore perfect, even as your Father which is in heaven is perfect."

Or, as he stated in Matthew 5:21-22, "Ye have heard that it was said by them of old time, Thou shalt not kill; and whosoever shall kill shall be in danger of the judgment, but I say unto you, That whosoever is angry with his brother without a cause shall be in danger of the judgment: and whosoever shall say to his brother, Raca [idiot], shall be in danger of the council: but whosoever shall say, Thou fool, shall be in danger of hell fire." It is obvious that Jesus *now* requires more.

Why is it that lifestyles like these were permitted in the Old Testament but disallowed in the New?

To Whom Much is Given

Moses allowed causeless divorce among the children of Israel "because of the hardness" of their heart. (Mark 10:4-6) But in the New Testament, hardness of heart is no longer excusable. In fact, because of the gift of the Holy Ghost and the availability of His great Grace, there is much more expected of God's people now than in previous dispensations.

"...for unto whomsoever **much is given**, of him **shall much be required**: and to whom men have committed much, of him they will ask the more." (Luke 12:48)

"For of the **grace God** that bringeth salvation **hath appeared** to all men. Teaching us that, denying ungodliness and worldly lusts, **we should live** soberly, righteously, and godly, in this present world; Looking for that blessed hope, and the glorious appearing of the great God and our Saviour Jesus Christ." (Titus 2:11-13)

"That in the **dispensation of the fullness of times** he might gather together in one all things in Christ, both which are in heaven, and which are on earth; even in him." (Ephesians 1:10)

"And hope maketh not ashamed; because the **love of God is shed abroad** in our hearts by the Holy Ghost which is given unto us." (Romans 5:5)

That God has committed great things of His Spirit and Truth to us in this dispensation is beyond question. Jesus said, "Blessed are the eyes which see the things that ye see: for I tell you that many prophets and Kings have desired to see those things which ye see, and have not seen them; and to hear those things which ye hear, and have not heard them." (Luke 10:23-24) That God would demand more, now that He has given more, is readily conceded by the Apostle Paul in Acts 17:30; "And the times of this ignorance God winked at; but **now** commandeth all men every where to repent."

God's True Feelings

While God—via Moses—suffered divorce, on occasion He would **vent his true feelings**. Just because He allowed divorce for innocuous cause does not mean that He liked it. His actual feelings on the matter are expressed in Malachi 2:14-16; "Because the Lord hath been witness between thee and the wife of thy youth, against whom thou hast dealt treacherously: yet is she thy companion, and the wife of thy covenant...Therefore take heed to your spirit, and let none deal treacherously against the wife of his youth. For the Lord, the God of Israel, saith that he **hateth putting away**: for one covereth violence with his garment, saith the Lord of hosts: therefore take heed to your spirit, that ye **deal not treacherously**." While God *permitted* divorce, in actuality He *hated* it.

Likewise, God suffered jewelry in the Old Testament, but on several occasions showed that He **was not for** His people wearing it.

Jacob and Jewelry

That God's children inherently knew how He really felt about jewelry is seen in Jacob's actions upon his return to the altar at Bethel and the subsequent 'housecleaning' that took place there.

Jacob had been with his uncle Laban for approximately twenty years in the land of Padan-Aram. While there, he took wives and had many sons and daughters. Upon his return to the land of Canaan he came back to Bethel and got-down-to-serious-business with God. He felt extremely pressed to do so as his estranged brother Esau was coming to meet him with four hundred armed horsemen. Jacob decided that this was a good time for an earnest prayer meeting.

"And let us arise, and go up to Bethel; and I will make here an altar unto God, who answered me in the day of distress, and was with me in the way which I went. And they gave unto Jacob all the strange gods which were in their hand, and **all their earrings which were in their ears**; and Jacob hid them under the oak which was by Shechem." (Genesis 35:3,4) It is a given that Jacob would put away all the "strange gods" in preparing his house to meet the One True God, but he innately understood that the jewelry had to go also.

It is important to note that it was *after* this act of consecration that God met Jacob in a manner that changed both his life and name forever. From that time of consecration and the subsequent meeting that followed, *Jacob; the "supplanter"* was known as *Israel; the "Prince with God"*.

Israel at the mount

After the children of Israel sinned and debauched themselves by forming and worshipping the golden calf, God commanded them to strip themselves of their ornaments. The jewelry Aaron used to make the calf had its source in Egypt—that in itself ought to make one question its acceptability with God. That it was used to form one of Egypt's *chief gods*—the calf—ought to make us consider even further its inappropriateness.

When Moses came down from the mount he heard the sound of music and saw the people dancing naked around the golden calf. In his anger, he broke the Ten Commandments that were hewed in stone and asked, "Who is on the Lord's side?" The Levites joined themselves with Moses cause and slew three thousand of the idol worshippers. It was immediately after that the Lord said unto Moses, "Say unto the children of Israel, Ye are a stiffnecked people: I will come up into the midst of thee in a moment, and consume thee: therefore **now put off thy ornaments from thee**, that I may know what to do unto thee." (Exodus 33:4-6)

It is here again that we see God's true sentiments concerning the ornamentation of His people. Though He had yet to give a specific commandment against the wearing of jewelry, we see by the nature of this verse that God did not like it, in spite of the fact that He suffered it.

Jewelry and Pride

"Moreover the LORD saith, Because the daughters of Zion are haughty, and walk with stretched forth necks and wanton eyes, walking and mincing as they go, and making a tinkling with their feet; Therefore the LORD will smite with a scab the crown of the head of the daughters of Zion, and the LORD will discover their secret parts. In that day the Lord will take away the bravery of their tinkling ornaments about their feet, and their cauls, and their round tires like the moon, the chains and the bracelets, and the mufflers, the bonnets, and the ornaments of the legs, and the headbands, and the tablets, and the earrings, the rings, and nose jewels." (Isaiah 3: 16-21)

Both the pride and the attire of the daughters of Zion are on display here. God declares that He is going to take them away—both the pride and the jewelry. It is interesting to note that God equated their prideful spirit with their jewelry in the same breath. No doubt it is because they **manifested their pride by their ornaments**, as well as in how they carried themselves. Though we know that pride can dress itself in rags, for the most part it does not do so if it can help it. Pride likes to manifest itself, and if it can afford it, it enjoys doing it through jewelry.

The Devil

The original prideful creature, the devil, was literally covered with precious stones or jewels. "Thou hast been in Eden the garden of God; every precious stone was thy covering, the sardius, topaz, and the diamond, the beryl, the onyx, and the jasper, the sapphire, the emerald, and the carbuncle, and gold: the workmanship of thy tabrets and of thy pipes was prepared in thee in the day that thou wast created. Thou art the anointed cherub that covereth; and I have set thee so: thou wast upon the holy mountain of God; thou hast walked up and down in the midst of the stones of fire. Thou wast perfect in thy ways from the day that thou wast created, till iniquity was found in thee." (Ezekiel 28:13-15)

That Lucifer was a beautiful creature is obvious. It is also obvious that he was lifted up by pride *because of his beauty, his brightness..* "Thine heart was lifted up because of thy beauty, thou hast corrupted thy wisdom by reason of thy brightness: I will cast thee to the ground, I will lay thee before kings, that they may behold thee." (Ezekiel 28:17)

The phrase "Thou hast corrupted thy wisdom by reason of thy brightness," (28:17) in the NIV reads this way; "…because of your **splendor**." In the NASV it reads; "…by reason of your **splendor**."

Seeing that *pride* was the instigating factor in turning the highest angel into the lowest devil, we should deeply desire not to partake of the same dread disease. If the jewels God bedecked that Arch *Angel* with, had *anything* to do with his later haughtiness, then it behooves us mere mortals to refrain from the spirit of ornamentation. God desires that His *people* be of a meek and quiet spirit, and adorned with a gentle and modest demeanor.

"But to this man will I look, even to him that is poor and of a contrite spirit, and trembleth at my word." (Isaiah 66:1-2)

"…and be clothed with humility: for God resisteth the proud, and giveth grace to the humble." (I Peter 5:5)

The Crux of the Matter

In the Old Testament God allowed the putting away of wives, though His nature loathed it. Now there is to be no divorce and remarriage except for the cause of fornication. In the Old Testament God simply said, "Thou shalt not kill." But in the New Testament a man is not to even be angry with his brother without cause, nor to call him a fool, lest he be in danger of hell. In the Old Testament it was, "Thou shalt not commit adultery." In the New Testament a man is not to even look upon a woman with lust in his heart.

Since we have now received much more *from* God, there is much more expected *by* God. In light of this, we see that, while in times past God suffered the children of Israel to wear ornamentation, He would on occasion let it be known that in reality—He did not like it. In the New Testament He makes this clear. The Apostle Peter, who spoke predominantly to Christianized Hebrews, writes;

"Whose adorning let it **not be** that outward adorning of plaiting the hair, and of **wearing of gold**, or of putting on of apparel; But let it be the hidden man of the heart, in that which is not corruptible, **even the ornament** of a meek and quiet spirit, which is in the sight of God of great price. For after this manner in the old time the holy women also, who trusted in God, adorned themselves, being in subjection unto their own husbands." (I Peter 3:3-5)

We do well to note that the main weight of the responsibility of the gospel to the Jews was committed to the Apostle Peter while the main weight of responsibility to the gentiles was laid upon the Apostle Paul.

"But… when they saw that the gospel of the uncircumcision was committed unto me, as the gospel of the circumcision was unto Peter—For he that wrought effectually in Peter to the apostleship of the circumcision, the same was mighty in me toward the Gentiles." (Gal 2:7-8)

The following injunction came from the Apostle Paul, and was intended mainly for the Gentiles Christians;

"I will therefore that men pray everywhere, lifting up holy hands without wrath and doubting. In like manner also, that women adorn themselves in modest apparel, with shamefacedness and sobriety; **not with** braided hair, **or gold, or pearls**, or costly array; But (which becometh women professing godliness) with good works." (I Timothy 2:8)

From both men, and to both groups came forth the same message against jewelry and ostentation. Surely these men can be trusted to know the mind of the Spirit and therefore what God now expects from His people.

May we again emphasize that while in the Old Testament, God would at times express His true feelings about jewelry—He never drew the line against it. Now, through both Peter and Paul… He has.

The troubling thing to me is that—in spite of the clear witness of scripture in both the Old and New Testaments—jewelry is making its way back into far too many churches that once knew better. This cannot be pleasing to God.

"For if I build again the things which I destroyed, I make myself a transgressor." (Gal 2:18)

The Adorning of the Harlot...

"And there came one of the seven angels which had the seven vials, and talked with me, saying unto me, Come hither; I will shew unto thee the judgment of the great whore that sitteth upon many waters: with whom the kings of the earth have committed fornication, and the inhabitants of the earth have been made drunk with the wine of her fornication. So he carried me away in the spirit into the wilderness: and I saw a woman sit upon a scarlet coloured beast, full of names of blasphemy, having seven heads and ten horns. And the woman was arrayed in purple and scarlet colour, and **decked with gold and precious stones and pearls**, having a golden cup in her hand full of abominations and filthiness of her fornication." (Revelation 17:1-4)

...vs. the Adorning of the Bride

"Let us be glad and rejoice, and give honour to him: for the marriage of the Lamb is come and his wife hath made herself ready. And to her was granted that she should be **arrayed in fine linen, clean and white**: for the fine linen is the righteousness of saints." (Revelation 19:7-8)

Compare the vast difference between the Lamb's bride and the mother of harlots. They differ in doctrine, righteousness, sanctity, spirit, demeanor—and in adornment. As part of the Bride of Jesus Christ, it behooves us to "walk worthy of the Lord unto **all pleasing, being fruitful in every good work**, and **increasing in the knowledge of God**." (Colossians 1:10)

What a difference a line can make.

Chapter Seven

Men's and Women's Apparel

Fallen mankind does not think like God, nor see things as God desires them to. This is true in every area of life, be it marriage and divorce, morality, entertainment, alcoholic beverages, correctness of speech, men's and women's hair, the upbringing and discipline of children, financial obligations to God (and each other), church attendance, views on the afterlife, sanctity of unborn lives, or how men and women ought to dress. It is certainly not the will of God for His people that know Him in Spirit and in Truth to live like those in the world that do not know Him.

"This I say therefore, and testify in the Lord, that ye henceforth **walk not as other Gentiles walk, in the vanity of their mind.** Having the understanding darkened, being alienated from the life of God through the ignorance that is in them, because of the blindness of their hearts." (Ephesians 4:17)

People who are lost walk in the vanity (or futility) of their minds, with an understanding that has been darkened by Satan and sin. The writers of the New Testament repeatedly remind us of this. Consider the following verses:

"I beseech you therefore, brethren, by the mercies of God, that ye present your bodies a **living sacrifice, holy, acceptable unto God,** which is your reasonable service. And be not conformed to this world: but be ye transformed by the renewing of your mind, that ye may prove what is that good, and acceptable, and perfect, will of God...Let love be without dissimulation. **Abhor that which is evil;**

cleave to that which is good." (Romans 12:1-2, 9)

"Be ye not unequally yoked together with unbelievers: for **what fellowship hath righteousness with unrighteousness? And what communion hath light with darkness? And what concord hath Christ with Belial?** Or what part hath he that believeth with an infidel? And what agreement hath the temple of God with idols? For ye are the temple of the living God; as God hath said, I will dwell in them, and walk in them; and I will be their God, and they shall be my people. **Wherefore come out from among them,** and be ye **separate**, saith the Lord, and **touch not the unclean thing**; and **I will receive you**." (2 Corinthians 6:14-17)

"**Casting down imaginations**, and every high thing that **exalteth itself against** the **knowledge of God**, and bringing into captivity **every thought** to the **obedience of Christ**." (2 Corinthians 10:5)

"That ye **put off** concerning the **former conversation** [lifestyle] **the old man**, which is corrupt according to the deceitful lusts; And be renewed in the spirit of your mind; And that ye put **on the new man**, which after God is **created in righteousness** and **true holiness**." (Ephesians 4:22-24)

"That ye may be **blameless and harmless**, the sons of God, without rebuke, in the midst of a crooked and perverse nation, **among whom ye shine as lights in the world**." (Philippians 2:15)

"...the carnal mind is not subject to the laws of God neither indeed can it be." (Romans 8:7)

"There is a way which seemeth right unto a man, but the end thereof are the ways of death." (Proverbs 14:12)

To live a life that is in tune *with* God, rather than one alienated *from* Him, we must understand all we possibly can about Him. We must have a desire to know what makes God glad and what makes Him sad.

What disappoints and disheartens God, and what makes Him rejoice.

The first step in obtaining this knowledge is—a tender heart. The knowledge of God will be repugnant to a heart of stone, and it is for this reason that God performs spiritual heart transplants. This is also the reason why conviction from God and contrite repentance towards God is imperative. This foreplay is necessary for a heart to be open to change, and must be followed by the infilling of the Holy Ghost. God pours out His spirit upon the repentant that we can maintain a tender heart towards Him instead of a cold, indifferent, dead heart of stone.

"And I will give them one heart, and I will put a new spirit within you; and I will take the stony heart out of their flesh, and will give them an heart of flesh: **That they may walk in my statutes, and keep mine ordinances,** and do them: and they shall be my people, and I will be their God." (Ezekiel 11:19-20)

"A new heart also will I give you, and a new spirit will I put within you: and I will take away the stony heart out of your heart, and I will give you an heart of flesh. And I will put my spirit within you, and **cause you to walk in my statutes, and ye shall keep my judgments,** and do them." (Ezekiel 36:26-27)

"Forasmuch as ye are manifestly declared to be the epistle of Christ ministered by us, written not with ink, but with the Spirit of the living God; not in tables of stone, but in fleshly tables of the heart." (2 Corinthians 3:3)

God desires to write His laws upon the tables of our tenderized hearts. As this is accomplished, there will be no area of life that a true child of God will keep back from His governing instruction—this includes the apparel we wear.

Is God Really Interested in What We Wear?

"And the eyes of them both were opened, and they knew that they were naked: and they sewed fig leaves together, and made themselves aprons...Unto Adam also and to his wife did the Lord God make coats of skins, and clothed them." (Genesis 3:7,21)

The fig leaves that Adam and Eve wore were not sufficient in the eyes of this holy God. We need to bear in mind that the leaves they used were good-sized. A few of them sewn together probably offered more covering than what a lot of people wear on the streets today. God therefore made them coats. He did not make them vests, mere aprons, tank tops or shorts. Rather, He clothed them completely, thus revealing that from the beginning of our history, **God is interested in what mankind wears.**

"The woman shall not wear that which pertaineth unto a man, neither shall a man put on a woman's garment: for all that do so are abomination unto the Lord thy God" (Deuteronomy 22:5). **God is interested in what mankind wears.**

"And thou shalt make them linen breeches to cover their nakedness; from the loins even unto the thighs they shall reach: and they shall be upon Aaron, and upon his sons, when they come in unto the tabernacle of the congregation, or when they come near unto the altar to minister in the holy place; that they bear not iniquity, and die: it shall be a statute for ever unto him and his seed after him" (Exodus 28:42-43). **God is interested in what mankind wears.**

"...And it shall come to pass in the day of the Lord's sacrifice, that I will punish the princes, and the king's children, and all such as are clothed with strange apparel." (Zephaniah 1:8) **God is interested in what mankind wears.**

"In like manner also, that women adorn themselves in modest apparel, with shamefacedness and sobriety; not with broided hair, or gold, or pearls, or costly array." (I Timothy 2:9) **God is interested in what mankind wears.**

***

There are people who like to think that God has no interest in what they wear—that such "trivialities" are beneath His concern. They even go so far as to denounce any teachings on the subject of dress as "legalism," often with great vigor and vehemence.

One such pastor and his church were hosting a meeting for like-minded people. The vast majority at this gathering had been in the past—teachers of Biblical holiness. Somewhere along the line however they had been (in their words) "liberated" from these teachings. Now, the major common denominator among them, almost their rallying cry, was to denounce all those who remained in holiness.

During the course of this convention the pastor received a phone call from Reverend I.H. Terry, his former pastor. After a few words of greeting, Brother Terry told the pastor that he wanted to come to the meeting and hold a public debate on the issues of men's and women's apparel and modesty. The pastor said that he would tell his fellows of Brother Terry's request—although he was obviously uncomfortable with even the thought of such a scene. Brother Terry then set forth rules that they would go by. The speaker from the antinomianism—that is, lawless—point of view would speak first. He would no doubt deride or try to explain away all scriptures concerning modest and separate dress for men and women, such as the ones given above as well as others.

Brother Terry then explained how he would conduct his defense of modest apparel for women. After about five minutes of discourse on the merits of Biblical modesty and explanations of the scriptures, the side door of the auditorium would open and in would come twelve dancing "women of the night," clad only in sheer nighties that leave little to the imagination. With arms linked, they would kick their legs in unison, doing a French can-can and singing the old Christian tune, "I'll Fly Away O Glory!" After about thirty seconds of this (with chaos and cries of shock among the congregation) some of the ushers would no doubt set about to show these ladies out the door. But the moment the first usher laid a hand on any one of them Brother Terry would scream into the microphone, "Get your hands off of that woman, you legalist! Show me chapter and verse where this is improper!"

After relating this little scenario to his former parishioner, Brother Terry then softly said over the phone; "You know, son, the only verses you have against a scene like that are the ones you were taught from childhood—the ones that you have now removed out of your Bible." To this the man had no answer and needless to say the debate did *not* take place.

What is Costly Apparel?

Some ask what Paul meant when he spoke against "costly array" in I Timothy 2:8. There are several different versions of answers to this, depending on whom you ask. One definition that must be considered is; if a person can only afford a $50 suit or dress and they are going into debt to buy $500 suits and dresses, then that is "beyond the pale" or obviously, *too* costly. But if $500 or $2000 is mere "pocket change" to someone of affluence, then such attire would be acceptable, as long as it was modest and properly covered the body. While the first definition is no doubt a scriptural truth let alone good sense, I can also follow the second line of reasoning—to a degree. There comes a certain point however where one has to draw a line, regardless of their income and say; "this is just *too* expensive as it is *too* ostentatious and pretentious." Where that line is exactly, I have no doubt that between a good conscience, a tender heart, the Holy Ghost and a conscientious Pastor, the honest saint can find it.

"Let us therefore follow after the things which make for peace, and things wherewith one may edify another." (Rom 14:19)

"We then that are strong ought to bear the infirmities of the weak, and not to please ourselves. (2) Let every one of us please his neighbour for his good to edification." (Rom 15:1-2)

***

For example, several years ago my wife and I were visiting the nation of Greece. At that time mink coats could be purchased there at relatively inexpensive prices—about 25 to 40% of what they were selling for in the United States. Many of our fellow-travelers (who were also Apostolics) were taking advantage of that. Some of their purchases may have been done for resale purposes—I cannot say—but I do know without doubt that some of it was not. However, it didn't matter to my wife and I what the cost of the coats were, or if they were being given away. We couldn't but feel that this apparel was definitely "costly" (no matter what the price), and could not therefore justify the purchase. Please don't judge us as being "holier than thou," as, again, I have lived long enough to see "pride robed in rags"—*and sometimes it wears rags on purpose.* But I also know that over the long haul of a lifetime our choices tend to either strengthen or weaken our brethren. And we must ever keep in mind, Rom 14:7:

"For none of us liveth to himself, and no man dieth to himself."

"We are not our own bosses to live or die as we ourselves might choose." (TLB)

The lines we draw in our personal lives make a difference in other peoples lives whether we believe it or not—especially if God has placed someone in a leadership position. And, **what a difference a line can make**.

The Rabbit Jacket

My wife once purchased a beautiful rabbit jacket—not mink—for $25 at a thrift store. We soon found that when she walked into churches, people's heads would turn because it really looked like a mink jacket. Whereas she did not feel to wear a sign around her neck that said, "Really folks, this is a rabbit jacket and I only paid $25 for it at a thrift store," she, within but a few services, quit wearing it and eventually got rid of it. My wife didn't take the attitude of some who say; "If they don't like it they can lump it. I have every right to wear this coat, as it does not fall under any category of impropriety." Instead, she followed the scriptural principle of caring for the brotherhood, putting their welfare first and striving not to be a stumblingblock.

"Him that is weak in the faith receive ye, but not to doubtful disputations. For one believeth that he may eat all things: another, who is weak, eateth herbs. **Let not him that eateth despise him that eateth not; and let not him which eateth not judge him that eateth: for God hath received him.** Who art thou that judgest another man's servant? to his own master he standeth or falleth. Yea, he shall be holden up: for God is able to make him stand. One man esteemeth one day above another: another esteemeth every day alike. Let every man be fully persuaded in his own mind. He that regardeth the day, regardeth it unto the Lord; and he that regardeth not the day, to the Lord he doth not regard it. He that eateth, eateth to the Lord, for he giveth God thanks; and he that eateth not, to the Lord he eateth not, and giveth God thanks. **For none of us liveth to himself, and no man dieth to himself.** For whether we live, we live unto the Lord; and whether we die, we die unto the Lord: whether we live therefore, or die, we are the Lord's. For to this end Christ both died, and rose, and revived, that he might be Lord both of the dead and living. But why dost thou judge thy brother? or why dost thou set at nought thy brother? for we shall all stand before the judgment seat of Christ. For it is written, As I live, saith the Lord, every knee shall bow to me, and every tongue shall confess to God. So then every one of us shall give account of himself to God. **Let us not therefore judge one another any more: but judge this rather, that no man put a stumblingblock or an occasion to fall in his brother's way.** I know, and am persuaded by the Lord Jesus, that there is nothing unclean of itself: but to him that esteemeth any thing to be unclean, to him it is unclean. But if thy brother be grieved with thy meat, now walkest thou not charitably. **Destroy not him with thy meat, for whom Christ died. Let not then your good be evil spoken of:** For the kingdom of God is not meat and drink; but righteousness, and peace, and joy in the Holy Ghost. For he that in these things serveth Christ is acceptable to God, and approved of men. Let us therefore follow after the things which make for peace, and things wherewith one may edify another. For meat destroy not the work of God. All things indeed are pure; but it is evil for that man who eateth with offence. It is good neither to eat flesh, nor to drink wine, nor any thing whereby thy brother stumbleth, or is offended, or is made weak. Hast thou faith? have it to thyself before God. Happy is he that condemneth not himself in that thing which he alloweth. And he that doubteth is damned if he eat, because he eateth not of faith; for whatsoever is not of faith is sin. **We then that are strong ought to bear the infirmities of the weak, and not to please ourselves. Let every one of us please his neighbor for his good to edification.** For even Christ pleased not himself; but, as it is written, The reproaches of them that reproached fell on me." (Romans 14:1-23, 15:1-3)

The Watch

Several years ago I purchased a watch from a minister for less than $50. It was a nice looking, heavy watch, so I bought it. One night I was sitting on the platform and my assistant pastor looked over and exclaimed, "Have mercy, you've got a Rolex!" I know this is hard to believe, but at that time I had no idea what prestige a "Rolex watch" was supposed to carry, nor what they sold for. However, I knew immediately that he was impressed. I said, "I doubt that it is a real Rolex. I only paid $50 for it from a brother." He said, "Boy, it sure looks like one." I soon found out that a 'cheap' Rolex is $1,200, while some sell for more than $10,000.

As time went on, three or four other people said, "Wow, you have a Rolex!" I would then go through the whole story, tell them it wasn't real, from whom I had bought it, and how much I had paid for it. One day it dawned on me that someday I would be teaching a financially-strapped husband and wife a Bible study. They might not even have food in their refrigerator and there I would be sitting, with this 'Rolex' glimmering in the sunlight. How would they know that the watch was a $50 fake? All they would be thinking is, "I have no milk in the icebox for my children, and this preacher comes to tell me about Jesus wearing a $2,500 Rolex."

I got rid of the watch. Not to prove I am better than anybody else, or because I think I'm extra holy, but because I don't want my "good to be evil spoken of." My desire was not to cast a stumblingblock in front of someone. I can live without a fake Rolex, and my wife can live without a rabbit coat. "Let your moderation be made known unto all men. The Lord is at hand" (Philippians 4:5). We need to be a moderate people. Yes, God does have concerns about this, or else *He would never have broached the subject in His word.*

No, I don't believe that we have to look like we just walked off of a Quaker Oats box, dressed in black and wearing wooden shoes. But I do believe that God desires His people to be without pride or ostentation. The beauty and allure of His people should be found in their attitude and in their spirit. Or as Moffet translates I Peter 3:3; "...with the immortal beauty of a gentle, modest spirit."

"Whose adorning let it not be that outward adorning of plaiting the hair, and of wearing of gold, or of putting on of apparel...." (I Peter 3:3)

"You are not to adorn yourselves on the outside with braids of hair and ornaments of gold and changes of dress...." (Mof)

"Your beauty should reside not in outward adornment...." (NEB)

"...Of the arrangement of the hair, that wearing of jewelry, or the putting on of dresses...." (TCNT)

[A pertinent question must here be asked: if jewelry is not condoned in scripture—which we have already studied in chapter 6—why is it okay for jewelry to be worn in the hair? Jewelry is after all... jewelry... regardless of *where* it's worn, be it the finger—the neck—the ear—or the hair]

"But let it be the hidden man of the heart, in that which is not corruptible, even the ornament of a meek and quiet spirit...." (I Peter 3:4)

"But rather that hidden personality of the heart, the imperishable ornament of a quiet and gentle spirit...." (Mon)

"Your beauty should, rather, be from within...it should be the inner loveliness of the heart, the imperishable jewel of a gentle and quiet spirit...." (NOR)

***

No matter how large a church becomes, any individual, from any walk of life should be able to come in and feel a warm reception from the saints. They should feel the presence of God's convicting power, and at the same time feel love from the people of God. Church is not meant to be a fashion show or a pageant on display. There should be a broad spectrum where doctors and lawyers, as well as dockworkers, welders and ditch diggers, can feel comfortable one with the other. Personally, unless the men of our local church are being used on the platform or are ushering, I don't care if they wear suits to church, or not. It doesn't bother me to have a mix of blue jeans and cowboy shirts with suits and ties, with everyone having genuine respect one for the other.

A few years ago, one Sunday morning, one of the roughest, toughest characters in our area walked into our church. For six years this man had hated me because I had baptized his wife in Jesus Name and she'd received the gift of the Holy Ghost. There were times when I think he would have killed me if he thought he could get away with it. As he sat in church that morning scowling, he began to look around and see that there were men in suits, white shirts and ties, *and* there were men in cowboy boots and Levis. He said to himself, "Hey, these are *men*. What are *men* doing in this church? This is supposed to be for old women." The more he looked around, the more "men" he saw.

The convicting Spirit of God gripped him that morning and he finally made his way down to the altar where he wept and sobbed for over an hour. While lying prostrate on the floor, he heard the voices of several men praying for him. When he finally looked up through his tears, he saw several pairs of cowboy boots around him. I baptized him in Jesus Name and helped pray him through to the Holy Ghost sitting at his kitchen table. Years later he is still a tremendous testimony to the saving power of God.

In that church there were scientific engineers, professional people, and a college professor. They all loved and felt very comfortable with each other. That is the way our Savior meant for it to be.

What is Modesty?

Webster's Dictionary definition of 'modest' is: "Observing conventional standards with regards to dress and behavior, not showy or ostentatious. Free from every trace of the lewd or salacious (which means arousing sexual desire or imagination)." Synonyms are: "chaste, clean, decent, pure, undefiled, unsullied, lacking all sign of pride, humble, meek, lowly, unassuming, not excessive in degree, moderate, reasonable, temperate, free from superficial embellishment, discrete, unadorned, undecorated, unpretentious."

It is the "lewd and arousing sexual desire or imagination" part of the definition that applies to godly teachings about sensuously high slits, wrap-around skirts (that aren't quite wrapped around) and any other alluringly provocative apparel, be it too revealingly thin or tight. It is not fair—let alone right—for women and girls in the church to wear clothing that arouses sexual desires. It is not 'fair' in that Christian men ought not to have to fight the same battles at church that they fight in the world and workplace. They should be able to come to the house of God and be free from that which the world displays. The Church house needs to be a refuge from the allures that the world is teeming with. While a visitor or new convert may not understand the principles of dressing modestly, a seasoned saint ought to know better. No one—either male *or* female—should ever lay stumblingblocks in the pathway of their brothers or sisters.

There are many subjects in the Word of the Lord that are worthy of teaching time and close, studious attention. I fear that far too many pastors take too much for granted when it comes to the saints—be they new converts—saved for many years—or raised in church—understanding and loving the principles of Biblical holiness and modesty. To take it for granted that because someone has obeyed Acts 2:38, they are going to automatically live up to God's declared principles, is wishful thinking indeed. There are a few people whom the Holy Ghost can change almost overnight, but most people need goodly amounts of Biblical instruction over goodly amounts of time. The days are all but completely passed when a person will do these things just because a minister 'says so.' People need to have an understanding of *why* we live the way we do.

"...and be always ready to give an answer to every man that asketh you a reason of the hope that is in you with meekness and fear." (I Peter 3:15)

Now and then, every church needs to take the time to go through the teachings of holiness. This is especially true as a church grows and new people come to the Lord. Pastors must stop and teach, lest the "beauty of holiness" slip away from the congregation. "Therefore we ought to give the more earnest heed to the things which we have heard, lest at any time we should let them slip." (Hebrews 2:1) Our desire should be that the church glorifies God in every way.

Women and Dresses

The question is often asked; "Why do your women always wear dresses?" There are several ways to answer this. One very good way is; "For the same reason our men always wear pants and do *not* wear dresses."

There was a time in our world when it was considered extremely out of bounds and contrary to nature for a woman to wear slacks (men's apparel). This was true throughout the whole of society and not just within religious spheres. And though we live in a culture where social mores are disintegrating daily—God's word never changes.

I have in my possession a 1957 single-frame cartoon of Dennis the Menace by Hank Ketchum. Dennis is looking at his mother, who is wearing slacks, and the caption says, "Aw, Mom, you don't look like a mother in them things." This cartoon joke wouldn't even be funny in our modern society. People of today would look at the cartoon, scratch their head and say, "I don't get it." But in 1957 it still struck a chord with the American people. Even then, there were many from all walks of American life, who had difficulty in accepting women who wore men's clothing. I also have a 1989 Dennis the Menace cartoon that shows Dennis gazing at his father, who is wearing a dress so that his mother can measure the hem. In the caption Dennis' dad angrily says, "Stop whistling at me!" Thankfully the humor still applies, since it is still not considered normal for a man to wear a dress. But due to the changes in our world, the 1957 cartoon makes sense only to those who can remember a different era, *or* to those who remember God's word! However, I would not be surprised that if the 1989 cartoon were to be run in the newspapers of today that Mr. Ketchum would be accused by some of 'gay bashing.'

In the past few years there have been several lawsuits in Great Britain and the United States filed by 'men' who wanted to wear dresses to work. When their bosses refused to let them do so, they cried discrimination because the companies allowed women to wear pants to work. As far as human (godless and Word-less) reasoning goes, they are entirely correct. If women can wear men's clothing why can't men wear women's apparel? But, to quote the old adage, "Two wrongs will never make a right."

Sometimes when dealing with a new convert or an immature saint, I pose the following scenario: "If you were to drive by my house and see me out in the front yard mowing my lawn in a dress, would you have a problem with that? If you had a friend or family member with you whom you were trying to win to God, would you point to me and proudly say 'there's my pastor?' I think not."

Thankfully, our culture is still *not quite* ready for that, although there are forces working overtime to head it in that direction. It behooves us to remember that even though society *has* accepted women wearing men's clothing, it still does not make it right in the sight of God. The voice of society is not the voice of God—and it never will be. Cultural acceptance does not equate with God's acceptance. "Thou shalt not follow a multitude to do evil...." (Exodus 23:2) However darkened the mind becomes, however alienated from God people get, if something is wrong—it is wrong. What is going to matter eternally is 'what does the Word of the Lord say?' When we stand before God we are not going to be judged according to what our neighbors did, or our friends and families thought, but by what is written in the sixty-six books called the Bible.

Abomination to the Lord

Long ago, God expressed His eternal opinion about cross-dressing of the sexes. "The woman shall not wear that which pertaineth unto a man, neither shall a man put on a woman's garment, for all that do so are abomination unto the Lord thy God." (Deuteronomy 22: 5) To ignore this injunction or sweep it under some mental carpet as being an archaic, Old Testament dictate, is to err greatly and gravely. God's outlook never changes. Our God is "...the same yesterday, today and forever." (Hebrews 13:8) Once something is *an abomination to God*, it is forever an abomination to Him.

There are many things that the Word of God calls abominations *unto the Lord*:

- Idolatry (Deuteronomy 7:25 and 27:15)
- Child sacrifice, fortune-telling and witchcraft (Deuteronomy 18:10-12)
- Prostitution and sodomy (Deuteronomy 23:18)
- Cheating and lying (Deuteronomy 25:14-16, Proverbs 11:10, 20:10, 20:23 and 12:22)
- A froward heart (Proverbs 3:32 and 11:20)
- The thoughts and ways of the wicked (Proverbs 15:8&9, 26)
- A proud heart (Proverbs 16:5)
- Murder and trouble-making (Proverbs 6:16-19)

An abomination to the Lord *never changes with time.* Men's and women's cross-dressing *is not even an issue of modesty*; it is a *moral issue with God.* Therefore, it *must* be so with us.

I once attended a conference in Salt Lake City with two fellow ministers. As we were eating in a restaurant one of them, who had just returned from the men's room said to me, "Booker, go to the restroom." I told him I didn't want to. He said, "No, man, go and tell me what you feel on the way in." This minister was a rather unique individual who always had a way of making life fun—so I went.

As I approached the restroom area to the left I saw a group of scantily-clad women who were brazenly watching every man who entered the men's room. There was, indeed, a 'foul feeling' as I went by them. One of them was wearing a bright red very tight dress, a long string of pearls and a smirk, and was swinging the pearls in a most provocative manner. It was a frightening... and then sickening sight as I realized that they were not women at all, but—transvestites. The realization that these were men made it truly an abhorrent sight. Honestly... I almost vomited.

I firmly believe that this is the way that God also feels about it, whether it be a man dressing like a woman, or a woman dressing like a man. Societies and their 'tolerance levels' may change but God does not change.

He "...is the same yesterday, today and forever" (Hebrews 13:8)

"For I am the Lord, I change not...." (Malachi 3:6)

He is "...the Father of lights, with whom there is no variableness, neither shadow of turning" (James 1:17)

It would do us well to pray that God would help us to 'feel the way He does' about every issue of life, and help us to 'see every issue as He sees it.'

Doing What's Right, in Spite of How we "Feel"

The scripture teaches us to "...resist not evil: but whosoever shall smite thee on the right cheek turn to him the other also." (Matthew 5:39) How many of us really *feel* like doing that when we are mistreated? But it doesn't matter what we *feel* like—we are to obey God regardless of what *our feelings* or *society* dictates. If someone treats us badly, we are instructed to "...bless them that curse you, do good to them that hate you, and pray for them that despitefully use you, and persecute you..." (Matthew 5:44)

We are going to be judged by what the Bible teaches, not by how we feel. God put us in this world to display Him. His written word must 'become flesh' and dwell within us. This is why we must "...receive with meekness, the engrafted word, which is able to save your souls." (James 1:21) It is not *our will* but *God's will* that ultimately has to be done. It is not our word but His word that must be obeyed. It is not our thoughts but His that must be acted upon. We cannot afford to be alienated from God by ignorant, hard and blinded hearts.

Every pastor will be called upon to give an account of the people he pastors (see Hebrews 13:17). Paul wrote "...what is our hope, or joy, or crown of rejoicing? Are not even ye in the presence of our Lord Jesus Christ at his coming? For ye are our glory and joy." (I Thessalonians 2:19-20)

Every pastor should deeply desire that his pastorate be pleasing to God. A church with 1,000 members who do not keep the commandments of the Lord is not pleasing to God. A church of 10 saints who are genuinely trying to reach the lost and who keep the commandments of God is pleasing to Him and vice-versa.

Every soul that comes to God is a soul that God is extremely interested in. He so loves the world that He clothed himself in human flesh and went all the way to Calvary to suffer, bleed and taste death. He came that we would not be alienated from Him, but might rather have tender hearts and teachable spirits.

Paul probably said it best when he wrote; "I therefore, the prisoner of the Lord, beseech you that ye **walk worthy of the vocation wherewith ye are called,** with all **lowliness** and **meekness,** with **longsuffering, forbearing one another in love**...." (Ephesians 4:1)

Chapter Eight

Men and Women's Hair

"For this cause we also, since the day we heard it, do not cease to pray for you, and to desire that ye might be filled with the knowledge of his will in all wisdom and spiritual understanding." (Colossians 1:9)

It is the desire of Jesus Christ that His people be filled with knowledge and understanding of what His will is in all things. This is imperative in order that they; "...might walk worthy of the Lord unto all pleasing, being fruitful in every good work, and increasing in the knowledge of God; Strengthened with all might, according to his glorious power, unto all patience and longsuffering with joyfulness." (Colossians 1:10)

The apostle Paul spoke to the elders of the church of Ephesus; "And how I kept back nothing that was profitable unto you, but have shewed you, and have taught you publicly, and from house to house. (Acts 20:20) And now, behold, I know that ye all, among whom I have gone preaching the kingdom of God, shall see my face no more. Wherefore I take you to record this day, that I am pure from the blood of all men. For I have not shunned to declare unto you all the counsel of God." (Acts 20:25-26)

Paul was clean from the blood of all men because he declared the whole counsel of God to men wherever he went. Furthermore he kept back *"nothing that was profitable."* He wanted men to walk worthy of the Lord unto all pleasing and have knowledge, wisdom and spiritual understanding that they might increase in the knowledge and grace of God.

Had the subjects of men's and women's hair *not* been profitable, Paul would not have taught the churches the will of God's concerning these matters. But this is obviously a subject God is keenly interested in and therefore moved on his apostles to deal with it.

"According as his divine power **hath given unto us all things that pertain unto life and godliness,** through the knowledge of him that hath **called us to glory and virtue**." (II Peter 1:3)

Ecclesiastes 4:12 tells us that a "three fold chord is not quickly broken." Throughout scripture we have many examples where intertwining facets (or cords) of truth when woven together and placed in our hearts have an ability to give strength that is not quickly dispelled. Whatever we can do to strengthen and enhance our walk with Him we need to learn and do. Any revelation of true holiness will enhance not only our worship but our lives. When one does not understand holiness unto the Lord their worship, however sincere, is going to be less than what God has planned for them or desires. A shocking example of this being Paul's statement to the Corinthians that it was possible to speak with the tongues of men and of angels and yet be as "sounding brass and a tinkling cymbal," because they did not understand nor possess the true love of God.

"I beseech you therefore, brethren, by the mercies of God, that ye present your bodies a living sacrifice, holy, acceptable unto God, which is your reasonable service." (Romans 12:1)

It is only reasonable that God (who saved our souls) expects us to present our bodies as a holy living sacrifice unto Him. One wonders just how far an individual has allowed God to have access to their soul, if they are not willing to allow Him access to their body as well. There is something about love, thankfulness and *submission* that goes a long ways towards us becoming the true saint that God wants us to be.

"I therefore, the prisoner of the Lord, beseech you that **ye walk worthy of the vocation** wherewith ye are called…" (Ephesians 4:1)

No conscientious Pastor, will shun to declare the whole counsel of God to the flock over which God has made him the overseer.

The Teachings

"Be ye followers of me, even as I am also am of Christ. Now I praise you, brethren, that ye remember me in all things, and keep the ordinances, as I delivered them to you. But I would have you know, that the head of every man is Christ; and the head of the woman is the man; and the head of Christ is God. Every man praying or prophesying, having his head covered, dishonoureth his head. But every woman that prayeth or prophesieth with her head uncovered dishonoureth her head: for that is even all one as if she were shaven. For if the woman be not covered, let her also be shorn: but if it be a shame for a woman to be shorn or shaven, let her be covered. For a man indeed ought not to cover his head, forasmuch as he is the image and glory of God: but the woman is the glory of the man. For the man is not of the woman; but the woman of the man. Neither was the man created for the woman; but the woman for the man. For this cause ought the woman to have power on her head because of the angels. Nevertheless neither is the man without the woman, neither the woman without the man, in the Lord. For as the woman is of the man even so is the man also be they woman; but all things of God. Judge in yourselves: is it comely that a woman pray unto God uncovered: Doth not even nature itself teach you, that, if a man have long hair, it is a shame unto him? But if a woman have long hair, it is a glory to her; for her hair is given her for a covering. But if any man seem to be contentious, we have no such custom, neither the churches of God." (I Corinthians 11:1-16)

In I Corinthians eleven, Paul's teaching concerns men and women's hair, and the power it has to bring either glory or shame to the individual. "Every **man** praying or prophesying, **having his head** *covered*, **dishonoureth his head**." (I Cor.11:4) The Greek word for dishonour is; *kat-ahee-skhoo'-no,* and means; "to *shame down, that is, disgrace* or (by implication) *put to the blush:*—confound, dishonour, (be a-, make a-) shame"

"But every **woman** that prayeth or **prophesieth with her head *uncovered* dishonoureth her head**" (Verse 5)

The key, pivotal verse of the entire chapter and discussion is verse number fifteen;

"But if a woman have long hair, it is a glory to her: for **her hair is given her for a covering**."

The word "covering" in the Greek; *peribolaion,* literally means "veil." The veil which the woman's Creator and Savior gave—is her long hair. Not only is it her "veil" it is also her "glory" as well as her sign of submission to God's established authority.

The Discussion

First and Second Corinthians are two of the most intriguing books of the New Testament. The amount of subject matter the apostle Paul covers in these letters is astounding. It seems that much of First Corinthians is dedicated to the answering of questions that had been put to the apostle Paul by the church. In the eleventh chapter he is apparently answering a question as to whether or not a woman should wear a veil, which was considered the proper thing in those days of Corinthian culture.

While we recognize local cultures as powerful entities, we must understand that bible truth transcends every culture, situation, circumstance and era. The Kingdom of Heaven has its own culture and while God is cognizant of the different customs between regions and nations of this earth, when His people are gathered from, "every kindred, and tongue, and people, and nation," (Rev.5:9) there will be but one culture and it will be based solely upon God's word.

Corinthian society of Paul's day considered an unveiled woman to be a lewd woman. Should not Christian women therefore wear veils? Paul's answer to them is; "Yes they should—but the veil they must wear, *regardless of any other*, is the veil which God has provided for them, that is; long, ie.—uncut—"But if a woman have **long hair**, it is a glory to her: for **her hair is given to her for a covering** (or veil)." (verse 15)[1]

Mankind has produced many types of veils throughout the world. Some veils cover part of the woman's face, while some cover the face entirely. Others may cover the entire face except for the eyes. Some veils are transparent, while some are mere hats. Others are no more than small handkerchiefs worn on the very top of the head. An interesting question to this is; "Which style of all these (if any) is a truly correct veil and most pleasing to God?" Many factions will gladly provide a host of opinions as to which they feel is the best.

But the veil which pleases God—is the one He ordained. This veil was provided by God to the very first woman, in the garden of Eden (before *any* clothing was to be found) and it has not changed with time, place or custom. Again—it is her "long hair."

Followers of Paul

The Apostle Paul wrote to the believers; "Be ye followers of me even as I also am of Christ." (I Corinthians 11:1) The only way one can follow Paul as he followed Jesus is to follow him through obedience to the word of God he gave us. How important is it to take heed to Paul's word—let alone the word of any other writer that God used? Paul's answer was stated to the Ephesian Elders when he said he was, "...*pure from the blood of all men*" as he had "*not shunned to declare unto you all the counsel of God.*" (Acts 20: 26-27) If Paul's hands were pure due to his deliverance of 'all the counsel of God,' how can our hands be pure if we refuse to obey "all the counsel of God?"

As an under shepherd of Christ's flock we also desire our hands to be clean from the blood of His people, in that we declare the self-same truth.

Keeping the Ordinances

"Now I praise you brethren that you remember me in all things, and keep the ordinances, as I delivered them to you." (I Corinthians 11:2)

These ordinances were given to us by the eternal God and are the oracles by which He rules the universe. We of this twenty-first Century are living in a society that does not care for laws, ordinances or rules. However, the God with whom we have to do, is not "running for office nor taking popularity polls." He simply expects to be obeyed.

Paul praised the Corinthians for remembering him in all things and keeping the ordinances as he delivered them. The J.B. Phillips translation puts it this way; "**I must give you credit for remembering what I taught you.**" Though the Corinthian church had many and severe problems, they were faithful in keeping much of the teaching that the apostle Paul brought to them.

We of this 21st century should also be diligent to keep the teachings of the apostles. It should be, that if Paul or any of the First century apostles attended a Jesus Name assembly of today, they would recognize it as one of God's churches and be pleased. Let is be said that we '… kept unchanged the rules which Paul delivered unto us.'

We read just how important this is in Revelation 22:18; "For I testify unto every man that heareth the words of the prophecy of this book, If any man shall add unto these things, God shall add unto him the plagues that are written in this book."

One cannot add to the word of God, nor take away from the word of God simply because it is not commodious to his lifestyle or taste. We must believe it and obey it.

The Witness of Headship

I Corinthians 11:3; "But I would have you know, that the head of every man is Christ; and the head of the woman is the man; and the head of Christ is God." This principle of headship is important indeed. We live in a society and world where talk of headship (or leadership) is not popular as it once was. However popular or unpopular it may be, it is still God's plan and therefore fundamentally important to keep in our minds.

"Every man praying or prophesying, having his head covered, dishonoureth his head. But every woman that prayeth or prophesieth with her head uncovered dishonoureth her head: for that is even all one as if she were shaven. (verse 4-5) In not keeping these ordinances we dishonour our Head, which is ultimately—God.

"For **the husband is the head of the wife, even as Christ is the head of the church:** and he is the saviour of the body. Therefore as the church is subject unto Christ, so let the wives be to their own husbands in every thing." (Ephesians 5:23-24)

"And hath put all things under his feet, and **gave him to be the head over all things** to the church, Which is his body, the fulness of him that filleth all in all." (Eph.1:22)

The Witness of Nature

"Doth not even nature itself teach you, that, if a man have long hair, it is a shame unto him?" (verse 14) It is forever settled in heaven and God's mind that it is a *shame* for a man to have long hair and *even nature* testifies to it.

Some have argued that while a "shame" may be bad, it is not necessarily a sin. It is interesting to note that the Greek word, *at-ee-mee'-ah*, that is translated into the word "shame" in I Corinthians 11:14, means; *infamy*, that is, (subjectively) comparative *indignity*, (objectively) *disgrace:*—dishonour, reproach, shame, vile. This exact same

Greek word (atimia) is translated as "_vile_" in Romans 1:26.

"And changed the glory of the uncorruptible God into an image made like to corruptible man, and to birds, and fourfooted beasts, and creeping things. Wherefore God also gave them up to uncleanness through the lusts of their own hearts, to dishonour their own bodies between themselves: Who changed the truth of God into a lie, and worshipped and served the creature more than the Creator, who is blessed for ever. Amen. For this cause God gave them up unto _vile_ affections: for even their women did change the natural use into that **which is against nature**: And likewise also the men, leaving the natural use of the woman, burned in their lust one toward another; men with men working that which is unseemly, and receiving in themselves that recompense of their error which was meet." (Romans 1:23-27)

This portion in Romans, God is dealing with homosexuality and lesbianism. Because people do not like to retain God in their knowledge, He can turn them over to "vile affections." The definition for the word "vile" used in this sense is "morally despicable, or contemptible because it is beneath minimal standards of human decency. Synonyms for the word "vile" are; base, despicable, ignoble, servile, sordid, squalid, wretched, offensive, atrocious, disgusting, evil, foul, hideous, horrible, horrid, loathsome, nasty, nauseating, obscene, repellent, repugnant, repulsive, revolting, sickening, and _icky_. Again, the Greek word for "vile" used to describe God's feelings about homosexuality is the exact same word He used to describe His feelings about a man having long hair.

***

At the age of 19 the author of this book came to God. He had long hair that came down to the bottom of his chest. Many of that generation thought long hair on men a "cool" thing. God however knew that it was a "vile" thing.

It was a drug and drink besotted hippie that went to the altar and sobbed for an hour and a half. It was also a young man that knew absolutely nothing about I Corinthians 11:14 and the spiritual baseness of long hair on men. All he knew for sure is that when he had finished repenting with anguished tears, his future pastor came to him, put his hand upon his shoulder and said, "Son, how do you feel?" He pulled his hair back out of his eyes, looked up at him and said, "I think I need a hair cut." His pastor knew that here was someone ready to be baptized in Jesus Name.

Where did he get those first words out of his mouth? He had no idea it was in the Bible but *nature itself* was beginning to talk with him. It is a beautiful thing to behold how things will begin to change in a life once a heart has been cleansed by God.

***

"But I would have you know, that the head of every man is Christ... **Every man** praying or prophesying, having his head covered, dishonoureth his head." (I Corinthians 11:3-4) A man praying with his head covered is dishonoring his head, which is Christ. Some other translations put it on this wise:

"If a man should pray or prophesy in the congregation with a veil over his head he would bring shame on his head." (Con)

"...Dishonours him who is his Head." (TCNT)

As for the **woman**;

"But every woman that prayeth or prophesieth with her head uncovered dishonoureth her head." (I Corinthians 11:5)

"...brings shame upon her head." (Knox)

"...is just as much a disgrace." (Phi)

"...diishonours her husband" (Tay) [As the husband is the head of the wife.]

"For that is even all one as if she were shaven."

"For it is one and the same thing as if she were shaven." (ASV)

***

A Time Life book of WWII displays a photo of Parisian women that had consorted with the occupational forces of the German army. These women's heads had been shaved and they were marched down the streets of Paris while their fellow Parisians jeered them. It was considered a great disgrace for these women's heads to be shaved because of their liaisons.

"But every woman that prayeth or prophesieth with her head uncovered dishonoureth her head: *for that is even all one as if she were shaved.*"

As far as God is concerned, an 'unveiled woman' is no better then the woman who had her head shaved. *It is vital to remember verse 15,* **God's veil for the woman is her long hair**. A woman's long, that is, uncut hair is the veil that God gives them. If her hair is cut:

"It is one as if she were bald." Verse 6 (Wyc)

"For if the woman be not covered, let her also be shorn" (KJV)

"If she cast off her veil, let her shave her head at once" (Con)

"but if it be a shame for a woman to be shorn or shaven, let her be covered." (KJV)

"if it is a foul thing to a woman to be poled or to be made bald, hide she her head." (Wyc)

The word "poled" means to cut off or shorten a growth, to clip or to shear. If it is a foul thing for a woman to be poled or to be clipped or to be sheared, it's the same as if she is made bald.

As for the man, the bible states he indeed ought **not** to cover his head, for as much as he is the image and glory of God. Man;

"has no need to veil his head" (Knox)

"he represents the likeness and supremacy of God" (Mof)

"but the woman is the glory of the man" (KJV)

"but a woman represents the glory of man" (Nor)

"the woman represents the supremacy of man" (Mof)

Furthermore, concerning "who came *first* in their relationship;

"For the man is not of the woman; but the woman of the man" (KJV)

"The first man didn't come from woman, but the first woman came out of man" (Tay)

At the risk of sounding "chauvinistic" in this Twenty-first century, may we state that the Woman was originally created for the sake of the man. **"Neither was the man created for the woman but the woman for the man"** (I Corinthians 11:9) **"For this cause ought the woman to have power on her head..."** For a woman to have the God given veil upon her head, that is her long hair, is a sign of her submission to authority.

"...A sign that she is under man's authority" (Tay)

"For this reason a woman ought to bear on her head an outward sign of man's authority" (Phi)

Then the apostle takes the teaching a step further. Woman ought to show this sign of her submission to authority:

"Because of the angels" (KJV)

"On account of the angels, if of nobody else" (Gspd)

"Especially out of respect for the angels" (Wms)

"Because of her (guardian) angels" (Mon)

"Because of the presence of the angels" (TCNT)

Angels take a keen interest in our efforts to walk with the Lord. They are interested if we are walking with Him in "all knowledge and all wisdom and with spiritual understanding." Angels are apparently interested in whether a man has his head uncovered and whether a woman has her head covered. Our submission to God is very important to them because they well remember fellow angels that were cast down out of heaven and bound by chains to the darkness of error. (See Jude vs. 6) The angels that fell loved not their first estate but left it and were cast down because of it.

Angels (both those who are faithful and fallen) watch God's Church closely. They know very well how God feels about insubordination and authority. As humans *and* members of the body of Christ we also need revelation of how God views submission and authority. When one is in submission to God it is as if they were under an umbrella of protection from untoward spiritual elements of this world. When people stray from His word they remove themselves out from under the umbrella of God's holy and spiritual protection.

Paul said, " be followers of me as I am of Christ." There is safety when one submits to leadership that submits to God. But there is delusion and deception in getting out from under proper leadership. It makes for a sad study to see how far and wrong people can go who remove themselves out from under God's counsel and commandments. "Because of the angels" a woman ought to have this power on her head.

Man is not to be independent of the woman, neither is woman to be independent of man. They need each other.

"Nevertheless neither is the man without the woman...For as the woman is of the man...even so is the man also by the woman." (KJV verse 11-12)

"For as the woman originates from the man, and all things originate from God...(NASB)

"But everything comes ultimately from God..." (Wey)

***

"Judge in yourselves: is it comely that a woman pray unto God uncovered?" (vs. 13 KJV)

How one answers this question of Paul's is very important, for the answer reveals where they are spiritually and in the knowledge of God and His word. If the answer is; "Yes, it is 'just fine' for a woman to pray uncovered, that is without a veil," that answer indicates ignorance of God's word or that there is error in the heart. If one knows what scripture teaches and yet persists in error, they declare plainly that they are wiser than God. They also make themselves judges of the word, and do not believe that the word will judge them. This attitude will never enter Glory where *only* His will is done. Matthew 6:10 states; "Thy kingdom come. Thy will be done in earth, as it is in heaven." " And there shall in no wise enter into it any thing that defileth, neither whatsoever worketh abomination, or maketh a lie: but they which are written in the Lamb's book of life." (Revelation 21:27)

If an individual can view these verses and declare that it is *not* comely for a woman to pray to God uncovered (that is without

God's provided veil—the woman's uncut hair) they show forth their faith in God and their desire to obey His word. As stated in Romans 2:7; "To them who by **patient continuance in well doing** seek for glory and honour and immortality, eternal life…"

Big doors swing on little hinges. I have never witnessed an Apostolic church break these scriptural mores and the glory of God continue to reside in it. Obedience to the word of God is a small price to pay for His abiding presence and Glory, let alone Heaven.

Did Jesus Have Long Hair?

Paul insists that Nature itself teaches that if a man has long hair, it is a shame—or vile—to him. Yet some have proposed that Jesus wore his hair long as justification for doing the same. If Jesus did have long hair Paul was caught in a grievous contradiction. In I Corinthians 9:1 he writes, " Have I not seen Jesus Christ our Lord?" Paul took a bold step indeed to declare it a vile thing for a man to wear long hair if he himself witnessed that Jesus Christ wore it long.

The truth is, Jesus did not have long hair, regardless of what the artists in the Renaissance period painted. A shallow study of history reveals that many of the Renaissance painters were at best bisexual. This is not a statement of bias but of historical record. These spiritually and morally troubled men depicted Jesus as having long hair, while the Holy men of God who spoke otherwise were "moved by the Holy Ghost."

It has been proposed that as Jesus was called a Nazarene he must have wore long hair because "Nazarites" of the Old Testament did so. This line of reasoning has no foundation whatsoever. That Jesus was raised in the city of Nazareth and was therefore called a "Nazarene" (Matthew 2:23) has no bearing on the "Nazarite vow" of Numbers chapter six. They are two *completely* different entities. The former is a title of anyone from a city called Nazareth while the other is a vow of separation defined by Moses.

***

Years ago the author was preaching at a church in the university town of Stillwater, Oklahoma. Not many people were there and as I spoke there entered a nice looking young man wearing a suit. After about ten minutes of speaking on a totally unrelated subject, I stopped and said, "I don't know why I'm saying this, because it doesn't fit anyone here... but it is a shame for a man to have long hair." I went on to discuss the belief of some that Jesus had long hair because He was a Nazarene, but that that was simply not the case.

In the book of Numbers 6:2-9 we read; "Speak unto the children of Israel, and say unto them, When either man or woman shall separate themselves to vow a vow of a Nazarite, to separate themselves unto the LORD: He shall separate himself from wine and strong drink, and shall drink no vinegar of wine, or vinegar of strong drink, neither shall he drink any liquor of grapes, nor eat moist grapes, or dried. All the days of his separation shall he eat nothing that is made of the vine tree, from the kernels even to the husk. All the days of the vow of his separation there **shall no rasor come upon his head: until the days be fulfilled, in the which he separateth himself unto the LORD, he shall be holy, and shall let the locks of the hair of his head grow. All the days that he separateth himself unto the LORD he shall come at no dead body**. He shall not make himself unclean for his father, or for his mother, for his brother, or for his sister, when they die: because the consecration of his God is upon his head. All the days of his separation he is holy unto the LORD. And if any man die very suddenly by him, and he hath defiled the head of his consecration; then he shall shave his head in the day of his cleansing, on the seventh day shall he shave it."

This is what is called the Nazarite vow. When a person took this vow, they were promising God that for a day, week, month, year, or in rare cases, a life-time, they would not cut their hair nor eat or drink any fruit of the vine, nor touch any dead body.

After that time period was over, the first thing that the man had to do

131

was shave his head. During the time he had the vow upon him and only during that time was he called a Nazarite. The fact that Jesus lived in the city of Nazareth has nothing to do with the Nazarite vow. Jesus therefore did not have long hair simply because he was of the city of Nazareth.

I spoke along that line of scriptural reasoning for about ten minutes, gave a brief testimony as to the long hair that I used to wear, and then went back to the message I had been delivering. After service the pastor asked me; "Do you know that young man that came in and sat down in the back of the church?" I replied that I did not as I had never been to Stillwater before. He said, "That young man lives in a religious commune on the outskirts of Stillwater. His hair is so long that it hangs to his waist. He had been invited to church by one of the members and he told them he might come to church tonight, but if he did no preacher was going to preach to him about his long hair."

Before the young man came to church he put on the dark blue suit and went and bought himself a shorthaired wig. He made it a point to come in late, and set in the back. As soon as service was over he approached the girl who had invited him and said; "You told him, you told him!" She avowed that she had not and actually had arrived to church late herself and didn't have a chance to speak to anyone. The Holy Ghost, who obviously was interested in and loved this young man very much, took the time to tell him some things he really needed to know.

"Isn't there a natural principle here, that makes us **feel** that long hair is disgraceful to a man." (11:14) (Phi)

"Does not nature itself teach you it is degrading for a man to wear long hair" (Wms)

Verse 15; "But if a woman have long hair, it is a glory to her." (KJV)

"But for a woman to have long hair is different; that is her pride." (Nor)

"…it is an added grace to her…" (Knox)

"for her hair is given her for a covering." (KJV)

"We feel this because the long hair is the cover provided by nature for the woman's head." (Phi)

"because her hair has been given her instead of a veil." (Mon)

Long hair is the veil that God has given to female gender of mankind. Men are not to cover their heads with long hair because it is to the glory of Jesus Christ. Women ought to have power (uncut hair) on their heads;

because of the angels,

because of the witness of nature,

because of what the word of God teaches,

because of the headship of Christ,

because of the headship of man,

and because of the Custom of the Church.

***

As to the last verse in this discourse—verse 16; "But if any man seem to be contentious,"

" seems anxious to dispute the matter…" (Ber)

"…we have no such custom, neither the churches of God." (KJV)

"… well, I acknowledge no other mode of worship…" (Mof)

"…I for my part recognize no other practice in worship than this…" (Gspd)

"…or in any of the congregations of God's people…" (NEB)

"…Nor yet the assemblies of God." (Rhm)

Concerning men and women's hair, the apostle Paul recognized no other mode of worship nor did he brook any contention over the matter. God's church (if it is indeed His church) will operate out of no other plan than this that he taught.

(Footnotes)

[1] Concerning the 'Second covering' teaching held by some—though I do not embrace it, I personally have no problem with those that do—*as long as the 'second covering' **never** replaces God's 'first'*—which is the woman's un-cut hair. When an individual believes—as some do—that wearing a 'man provided veil' gives allowance for a woman to cut her hair, they are guilty of what Peter warned of in his second epistle concerning Paul's writings (in this case…men and women's hair and the veil); "*As also in all his epistles, speaking in them of these things; in which are some things hard to be understood, which they that are unlearned and unstable wrest, as they do also the other scriptures, unto their own destruction.*" (2 Peter 3:16)

Chapter Nine

Facial Hair on Men

I approach the subject of beards and mustaches carefully, knowing that God's word is silent as to whether or not a man should wear them. Rather, it reveals that the men of Israel during the time of Moses wore beards, as did other Biblical characters. (Leviticus 13: 29-30)

Some men that we know had beards were:

- Aaron, the first High Priest (Psalm 133:2)
- David's men who were sent to comfort Hanan the Ammonite upon the death of his father (II Samuel 10:4-5)
- Amasa, the short-lived captain of David's host (II Samuel 20:9)
- Mephibosheth, the son of Jonathan (II Samuel 19:24)
- Ezra (Ezra 9:3)
- Ezekiel (Ezekiel 5:1)
- and (debatably) our Lord Jesus Christ (Isaiah 50:6)

The United Pentecostal Church has (in the main) for the last several decades, been opposed to beards and mustaches on men. Generally speaking, this stand has been taken in an effort to not be identified with elements of the world that are less than desirable: most notably the "beatniks" of the late forties and fifties, the "hippies" of the sixties and early seventies, and various carry-over elements that are alive and well.

Facial hair on men is now becoming a point of controversy within the ranks of many today—and not just Pentecostals. While being clean-shaven is still the generally-accepted code among our assemblies, there has been in recent years, in some congregations, a resurgence of men wearing a mustache, beard, or both.

I have neither the time nor the inclination to do an in-depth study in this book into the *history* of facial hair on men. Such a study might be interesting, but it would prove little and settle nothing. Although I personally do not and would not wear either a beard or a mustache—and have not had them in the churches I have pastored—I do not believe that it is a "heaven or hell" issue—unless a person allows a rebellious attitude over it to take root in their heart.

But I honestly do feel that our churches are definitely better off when our men do not wear them... and I dedicate the remainder of this chapter to express my reasons why.

The best way for me to relate my view on this subject is to tell the story of an incident that took place while I was evangelizing. We were holding a lengthy revival in Bakersfield, California for the great church then pastored by I.H. Terry. We had been in revival for about three weeks, when one day a young man with a full beard knocked on my trailer door. He wondered if he could ask me a question and I replied that, "yes, he certainly could." He proceeded to take his beard in one hand and pointing at it with the other asked; "Is this beard going to send me to hell?"

After a shocked moment or two I replied, "Why in the world are you asking me this question?"

He answered, "Because there's an old man in this church who told me this beard is going to send me to hell, and that he can give me chapter and verse to prove it."

"Was it the pastor?" I asked (because if it was, I was sending him straight to Brother Terry).

"No, it's the old fellow who takes care of the flowers," he replied.

Relieved, I asked, "Who are you and what is your association to this church?"

"I started coming here about six weeks ago and was baptized in Jesus' Name," he answered.

"I've been in revival here for three weeks. Why haven't I seen you before?" I queried.

"I quit coming because of this beard thing," He said.

At this point I invited him into my trailer, knowing that this young man was at a great cross road in his life and that it must have taken a lot for him to even knock on my door.

I proceeded to ask him if he understood why he was baptized in Jesus' Name.

"Yes, it was for the remission of my sins."

"Do you know why the Name of Jesus was used rather than the titles, 'Father, Son and Holy Ghost?"

"Yes, because Jesus is the Name of the Father, and it is the name of the Son and Holy Ghost—and that these are merely manifestations of the One God."

I was impressed, and went on to ask him; "Do you have the Holy Ghost?"

"No," he replied.

"Do you know what it is?"

"Well, I know that when I get it I'll speak in other tongues."

I could see that this young man had a good perception about initial salvation. So, I slowly said, "Well, son, it is my personal opinion that Jesus could very well have had a beard. It is also probable that some of the apostles had beards, as well as many Old Testament heroes. I hope they were saved, don't you?"

He perked up and replied, "Yeah... Yeah!"

"But you know," I continued, "we are not living in the Middle East 2,000 years ago. We are in America in the latter part of the 20th century, and we are doing our best to win people to Jesus. Now, as far as God is concerned, there are only three types of people in the world: Jews, Gentiles and the Church of God. In I Corinthians 10:32 Paul stated his desire to not offend the *Jews, Gentiles, nor the church....* One thing is for sure; we in our society and time should do our best to not offend anyone within those groups... for the sake of the gospel's effectiveness."

I then read to him Mark 8:35 "For whosoever will save his life shall lose it; but whosoever shall lose his life for my sake **and the gospel's**, the same shall save it."

Then I read Mark 10:29-30: "And Jesus answered and said, Verily I say unto you, There is no man that hath left house, or brethren, or sisters, or father, or mother, or wife, or children, or lands, for my sake **and the gospels**, but he shall receive an hundredfold now in this time...."

I pointed out that in both of these scriptures Jesus makes reference to a person either "losing his life," or leaving something of great personal value for "my sake and **the gospels.**" Jesus is subtly, but definitely, revealing that there is a difference between what we do for *His sake* and what we do for the *sake of the gospel.*

An example of this difference is found in Acts chapter 15, over the issue of whether or not the Gentiles had to be circumcised according to the Mosaic Law in order to be saved. After much discussion and a conference in Jerusalem, it was decreed that the Gentiles did not have to be circumcised, "For it seemed good to the Holy Ghost and to us...." [this verse and principle was discussed in greater detail in Chapter 3]

Paul, Silas and Judas then began to make their way among the Gentile churches, reading the decree that loosed them from the ritual of circumcision. The believers rejoiced—the men no doubt being greatly relieved—and got back to the business of having revival.

At this point, an amazing thing took place. In the very next chapter, Acts 16, Paul passed through the city of Lystra and found a disciple there named Timotheus, whose mother was a Jew but whose father was a Gentile. In verse 3 we read, "Him would Paul have to go forth with him; and took him **and circumcised him** because of the Jews which were in those quarters; for they knew all that his father was a Greek."

Paul, who had just gone head to head with the judaizers of Jerusalem over the subject of circumcision, now takes Timothy and circumcises him. This he does while at the same time teaching, yea demanding that circumcision after the law of Moses is not necessary.

Obviously, Timothy did not subject himself to this ordeal in order to be saved. He understood Paul's teaching that New Testament circumcision is accomplished through repentance and baptism in Jesus' Name. "And ye are complete in Him which is the head of all principality and power: In whom also **ye are circumcised** with the circumcision made without hands, in putting off the body of the sins of the flesh by the circumcision of Christ: **Buried with Him in baptism....**" (Colossians 2:10-12) Why then would Timothy submit to an excruciating rite that no longer had any spiritual significance or merit? He did it not for "Jesus' sake" but for the *"sake of the gospel."*

Paul—and now Timothy—were doing their best to reach the lost, both Jew and Greek. Paul no doubt felt that because Timothy's mother was Jewish and that many Jews of that region knew that his father was a Greek, their cause would be advanced and reception to the gospel increased—if he were circumcised. It was not a case of right or wrong, truth or error, heaven or hell. It was a case of doing what was *best* in their time, place and society to reach souls for Jesus Christ.

To the Hebrews who had embraced this tenet of Mosaic Law, the thought of an uncircumcised Jew was abhorrent. For this same Jew (Timothy) to tell them that unless they embraced Jesus as their Messiah, were baptized into His name and received His Spirit they were a lost people, would be more *than some* could handle. Paul realized this and knew that for the expediency and acceptance of the Gospel, Timothy should submit himself to physical circumcision for the sake of others being more open to the truth and therefore saved.

At this point in the narrative I said to my young visitor, "Son, do you see those houses across the street? If you were to take your Bible, knock on those doors and say to whoever answered, 'I want to share with you a revelation that God has given to me about baptism in Jesus Name,' some of those people would slam the door, turn inside and say 'Some hippie is out there peddling trash.' However, were you to shave your face and have a nice, wholesome appearance, chances are that the same people might slam the door in your face and say, 'Some *guy* is out there peddling trash.' They still might not receive the gospel, but at least they could not throw off on your appearance and use it for an excuse not to listen to you. Again, we are not living 2,000 years ago in the Middle East. We are in America, in an entirely different society. Not *everyone* in our world is comfortable with facial hair on men, but—*no one minds if a man is clean-shaven.*"

After thoughtful consideration he looked at me and said, "What you are telling me is that, while my beard is not a sin, it could be a stumblingblock to some people. Now that I can understand." I could have kissed him (*but I didn't*).

I answered that that was exactly what I was saying, and then asked him this question, "Son, which is easier for a man to do: be circumcised for the sake of the gospel, or shave his face?"

He looked at me for a long time, rubbed his beard, and then said, "I think I will go home and shave."

That night he came to service with the beard shaved off, but he still had a mustache. He stood to testify and, while rubbing his chin, said, "Church, please be patient with me. As you can see, I am working on it. I really do want to live for God." Everyone laughed and rejoiced.

The last night of revival he came with his mustache shaved, and received the gift of the Holy Ghost. Through the years, whenever we see each other at various conferences, he always rubs his clean-shaven face and laughs.

It will be good to be with this unselfish man in Heaven, and to be with the souls that he has won to God through the years. Some of them will probably be there because he was willing to take a step of self-sacrifice for—*"the sake of the gospel."*

What *They* See is What *You* Get

It is perhaps profitable to take a moment here to speak of those people in a church whose lifestyle—and appearance speaks every bit as loud as does the voice of the pastor. It is those people *who the pastor has placed in 'high leadership' and on the platform on a steady basis.* I am speaking of singers, choir members, service directors, assistants and their wives, secretaries, board members, youth leaders, Sunday School directors, etc. etc. People that are *visible,* and used in leadership set a very powerful example to all other members of the flock as to what is *really expected of them.* And people are not 'dummies.'

One of the most grave mistakes a pastor can make is to underestimate the 'thinking capacity' of the people he pastors. Ps. 119:130, states; "The entrance of thy words giveth light; it giveth understanding unto the simple." People are not going to receive 'the entrance of God's Word' year after year and remain bereft of 'understanding.' When they see on a consistent basis that only those who align themselves with the teachings of their pastor are used consistently—they will 'get the message' that this is what is expected.

To preach and teach that it is not best for a man to wear facial hair and then allow ushers and choir members and board members to have them is ludicrous. Actions still speak louder than words. This is true across the board with all 'standards' of holiness and separation, be it, television, jewelry, make-up, cut hair on women, long hair on men or whatever the case may be. When it comes to the 'long haul' of what a pastor want the church to become... 'What *they* see is what *you* get.'

Jacob and the Spotted and Speckled

In Genesis 30:31 Jacob's father in law, Laban asked him "What shall I give thee?" He asked this in response to Jacob's accusation that Laban had changed his wages ten times and had not done him 'right' by way of remuneration.

Jacob's answer was; "Thou shalt not give me any thing: if thou wilt do this thing for me, I will again feed and keep thy flock: I will pass through all thy flock to day, removing from thence all the speckled and spotted cattle, and all the brown cattle among the sheep, and the spotted and speckled among the goats: and of such shall be my hire. So shall my righteousness answer for me in time to come, when it shall come for my hire before thy face: every one that is not speckled and spotted among the goats, and brown among the sheep, that shall be counted stolen with me." (vs.31-33)

"And Laban said, Behold, I would it might be according to thy word." (vs. 34)

It is very important that we understand exactly what is going on and what Jacob did to correct it. The 'new deal' between he and Laban was that from 'here on out' only the spotted, speckled and ringstraked, sheep, goats and cattle would belong to Jacob, while all of the white or solid colored of the flocks and herds would belong to Laban. When Jacob offered this arrangement to Laban, he apparently 'leaped at it' as he knew there was nary a spotted or speckled among the bunch. No doubt he thought as did P.T. Barnum did much later, "There's a sucker born every minute."

But Laban underestimated Jacob as well as Jacob's God. The scripture goes on to tell us that; "...Jacob took him rods of green poplar, and of the hazel and chesnut tree; and pilled white strakes in them, and made the white appear which was in the rods. And he set the rods which he had pilled before the flocks in the gutters in the watering troughs when the flocks came to drink, that they should conceive when they came to drink." (vs 37-38)

We then read one of the most telling verses of the entire narrative; "And the flocks conceived **before the rods**, and **brought forth cattle ringstraked, speckled, and spotted**." (vs.39) Scriptures go on to relate through verses 40-43;

"And Jacob did separate the lambs, and set the faces of the flocks toward the ringstraked, and all the brown in the flock of Laban; and he put his own flocks by themselves, and put them not unto Laban's cattle. And it came to pass, **whensoever the stronger cattle did conceive, that Jacob laid the rods before the eyes of the cattle in the gutters, that they might conceive among the rods.** But when the cattle were feeble, he put them not in: **so the feebler were Laban's, and the stronger Jacob's. And the man increased exceedingly**, and had much cattle, and maidservants, and menservants, and camels, and asses."

We must ever remember when reading this narrative what the Apostle Paul admonishes in 2 Tim 3:16-17; **"All scripture is given by inspiration of God, and is profitable for doctrine, for reproof, for correction, for instruction in righteousness: That the man of**

God may be perfect, throughly furnished unto all good works."

What the Patriarch Jacob did was written for our instruction. While I do not pretend to understand it, when it came to the flocks and herds of Laban—what was *set before them* when it came time to drink and conceive—is what they produced. Pastor take note—what is set before the flock, by way of platform and leadership—is what the congregation will eventually become. Jewelry laden, Hollywood watching, immodest choirs, singers and leaders will produce "after their kind." (Genesis 1:21, 1:25, 6:20, 7:14) And the sanctuary, i.e. 'altar and congregation area' is where most of our 'spiritual watering and conceptions' take place. And Pastor, regardless of what you preach, when all is said and done; **What *They* See** (the congregation sees by way of platform and leadership) **is What *You* Get** (is what the congregation eventually becomes).

Having said that—and believing it—I want to re-emphasize the statements made in chapter 3; saints… should never take on the role of the pastor or become the "FBI of Pentecost." Saints must always let the pastor be the pastor. He must be allowed time and space to deal with people and problems. Although at times it may seem like the pastor is not 'on top of things' or doesn't know what is going on, that still does not give anyone else pastoral authority. He may be dealing with the problems but not announcing that fact to the world. Maybe it has already been dealt with, or maybe he is in the process of feeling out exactly what to do. At any rate, saints should be glad they are not the ones who will have to stand before God in judgment.

I repeat this statement because when it comes to handling people and their problems the Pastor has the ultimate responsibility—and no one else. Sometimes it may look like someone in leadership or on the platform is 'getting by' with something, when again; 'you may not be seeing the pastor's doctrine…merely his longsuffering.' A pastor must have a free hand to deal with problems as he deems necessary.

A very wise and good pastor friend of mine related to me how that years ago their was a girl in his church who played the piano for the majority of church services. He had found out that she had not been doing well at all and had actually 'run afoul' of several tenets of the church. He had determined that she must be removed from being a musician until she could get a hold of God as well as herself. But the night before he was going to call her into his office and relieve her of her duties as a musician, he had a dream that he knew was from the Lord. In the dream he saw this young lady caught in a savage whirlpool and being pulled down below the surface of the water. Every now and then however he would see her head bob to the top. As the pastor rushed to where she was he could see that she was hanging on to something as she swirled around and round in the water. It was the only thing that was keeping her afloat—and it was the keyboard of a piano.

The pastor awoke from his dream and knew that were he to remove her at that particular time, she would no doubt 'sink and be lost.' He and his wife continued to patiently work and pray with the young lady and it was not very long before she caught herself and is still doing a fine job of living for God today.

So, a word to those who feel the great need to 'help the pastor' in this business of pointing out the errors of others, a word from James is probably in order;

"My brethren, be not many masters, knowing that we shall receive the greater condemnation." (James 3:1)

"Dear brothers, don't be too eager to tell others their faults, for we all make many mistakes; and when we teachers of religion, who should know better, do wrong, our punishment will be greater than it would be for others." (Tay)

Chapter Ten

Modern Technology

I preface this chapter with a rather strange statement. Though this portion of the book is directed to the subject of 'Modern Technology' and its tremendous potential for both good and evil, I must state from the beginning that I am able to offer little by way of advice as to what ought to be done with every technological innovation that comes along. We *do* know that innovations are coming faster than we ever dreamed possible. Each passing day offers greater opportunities to do more for God or for the devil. Every God-fearing pastor and saint is going to have to work out for himself or herself what devices should to be allowed in the home or workplace.

Regardless of the technology we choose to use, the accessing of pornography or Hollywood type entertainment *should never once be named among us*. Nor should a child of God risk diving into the unknown, dangerous waters of 'chat rooms' or indulge the extravagant waste of our most precious commodity—time. As these very important decisions are made, it would no doubt be better to err on the side of being too careful rather than be too indulgent.

Again, let me say that I do not claim to have the answers nor have I yet to meet anyone with all the answers. I have met some who thought they had them, but upon close inspection, and after a few pointed questions, we both knew that they really didn't know either. In addressing this subject I therefore place myself in a "No Win" situation—for no one will be completely happy with my every statement or conclusion...including myself. All we can do is try. I offer only 'food for thought' to both the conscientious and the conscienceless. If we can somehow be made stronger in our purpose to strengthen our fellow man, protect our church and family, and not defile ourselves, this effort will not be in vain. And, I know of no other way to begin this endeavor except to simply 'plod through it a step at a time.'

Two verses (among many) that should ever be kept in mind and practice are:

"The integrity of the upright shall guide them: but the perverseness of transgressors shall destroy them." (Proverbs 11:3)

"The just man walketh in his integrity: his children are blessed after him." (Proverbs 20:7)

Where We Are

Technologically, the journey from where man was when Jesus Christ walked the earth has been a long, slow advance until the last half century. It has been said that it took from the days of Christ until the beginning of the eighteenth century to double the amount of mankind's collective knowledge that was possessed back then. That amount of knowledge was doubled within the next 200 years— from 1700 AD to approximately 1900 AD. Now, it is said, that the entirety of mankind's knowledge doubles every two years, and some say that with the oncoming 'nano-technology' it will be doubled every six months. No doubt Daniel's prophecy made over 2,500 years ago is now being fulfilled; "But thou, O Daniel, shut up the words, and seal the book, even to the **time of the end**: many shall run to and fro, and **knowledge shall be increased**." (Daniel 12:4)

While knowledge has increased dramatically, and we marvel at the wonders of our 'information age,' the fabric of man and society unravels at a rival pace. Nor has the church been left unscathed in this process. We are inundated daily with reports of both victories and failures in the realms of technological use. Conscientious pastors that desire the lost to be saved and the saved to stay saved are grasping for answers to give to both. Whatever conclusions we come to, it is a comfort to know that 2,500 years ago, the Spirit (through Daniel) knew we would be here. It must also be brought to our attention that some of these problems did not arise just yesterday.

From the Printing Press to...

In 1444 Johannes Gutenberg invented a 'machine' that would forever change the world: the printing press. The first thing it was ever used for was the printing of the Bible, without which the Reformation would have been impossible. The long, arduous process of getting the Word of God into the hands of the common man produced effects felt to this very hour. Alas, as we all know, the Bible has not been the only thing printing presses have been used for. Literature that runs the gamut from John Bunyon's Pilgrim's Progress to porno's vile productions have been the result of this breakthrough technology. Crude as Gutenberg's original design was, it was the opening of the door to where we are today, both in things good and bad.

Billy Sunday vs. Modern Technology

Around 1905, America experienced the phenomena of a Presbyterian evangelist by the name of Billy Sunday. The full impact of his ministry was felt from 1914 (the beginning of W.W.I. in Europe) until a year after the end of "Great War." Those who have lived only in the last half of the Twentieth-Century cannot conceive the era or impact which Billy Sunday had upon this nation. I used to visit with an elderly lady who heard him speak when she was a girl. She stated that it was an experience one could never forget.

Until that time, life in America was much as it had been throughout the nineteenth century. For the most part Americans were a rural people, with rural 'old fashioned' values. Even the majority of city dwellers knew first hand the experience of sitting out on a porch in the evening, visiting with neighbors, trading recipes and inquiring into the health of various friends and family. Much time was spent in these and like activities as time was in relative abundance. We were not yet a harried, hurried people as the vast majority of our labor and time saving devices were yet to be invented.

Telephones, though they were being marketed, were by no means wide spread. Indeed, when President Rutherford Hayes had one installed in the White House in 1880, the only other phone he could call in all of Washington D.C. was the lone phone in the Treasury Department. And it was not until 1922 that Warren G. Harding was able to have a radio placed in the White House. Therefore, the society that Evangelist Sunday affected was a very different one from ours today… but affect it he did.

One of the nicknames given the Eighteenth Amendment of the U.S. Constitution (Prohibition of the sale of alcoholic beverages) was the "Billy Sunday Amendment." This was due to his powerful influence in getting it passed. Influence accomplished only through preaching. His biography, "Sawdust Trail Preacher, Billy Sunday" states that just one of his sermons; "Mr. Booze" closed down over 460 bars in the state of Illinois alone—almost 'overnight.'

To imagine the impact Billy Sunday had on America one has merely to look at the demands he placed upon a city in order to come and hold a crusade. Included in his list of obligations:

1. He must receive an invitation, signed by every Protestant minister within the city before he would consent to come.

2. While the crusade was in progress, be it for six weeks or six months, not one of these ministers were to preach from his own pulpit. During the duration of Mr. Sunday's stay, his was to be the only preaching voice heard in that city.

3. A tabernacle or wooden coliseum must be built as near to the center of the downtown area as possible. It must seat at least ten

thousand people, preferably, twenty thousand.

4. Services were to be held daily, both day and night with the offerings being used to reimburse the churches for expenses incurred. The last night's offering went to Sunday and his entourage. (This offering was such a huge affair and received so much criticism that many people came that night just to watch the process)

One would be hard pressed to imagine any religious figure today getting away with these demands. Anyone who would dare make them would be laughed at, if not driven out of town. Nevertheless, not only were Evangelist Sunday's demands met, both governmental and ministerial leaders in city after city would plead for him to come and preach to their people. Many times he would be met by a parade, with government officials, ministers and citizens alike waving flags, hoisting banners and cheering their appreciation of his coming. If it was a major city (such as Philadelphia) it was common for over 100,000 people to come out and hear him preach.

Billy Sunday did not deliver the New Birth message of Acts 2:38 salvation, but he was a hard hitting, sin naming, exuberant preacher who had an uncommon knack for making crooked officials and lazy preachers extremely nervous. He also had the ability to get people to come 'down the sawdust trail' (walk down to the front of the sawdust strewn tabernacle) and 'give their heart to the Lord.' It is estimated that the 'conversions' were in excess of one million people. As was stated, the most impacting years of his ministry were from 1914 to 1919, when he held his greatest meetings in America's largest cities.

But after the First World War it all began to change. Gradually the crowds and interest began to diminish, and the cities and ministers were no longer interested in meeting Sunday's demands. From 1921 until his death in 1935, Sunday was eventually reduced to speaking to (for the most part) smaller, rural churches.

What Happened?

Until the day he died, nothing in Billy Sunday's ministry changed in either content or delivery. While he grew a little slower as he grew older, the sharp decline in his popularity had nothing to do with that. What had changed was…America.

In the book, "Sawdust Trail Preacher, Billy Sunday," it is stated that three things brought down the ministry of Billy Sunday:

Radio… *people no longer had to leave their homes for entertainment.*

Cars… *they could now afford to travel easily and 'get away.'*

Motion Pictures… *a whole new world of 'pleasure' was opened up, and they could escape their troubles and be entertained by entities other than God.*

With this in mind, we see that America's '*spirituality*' has suffered for many decades due to its hunger for 'gadgetry' more than its hunger for God. In a very real sense, modern technology has helped mankind along the road to fulfilling II Timothy 3:1-5 "This know also, that in the last days perilous times shall come. For men shall be lovers of their own selves…**lovers of pleasures more than lovers of God.**"

While a great many people, both within the church and without, have recognized the obvious and subtle dangers of the Hollywood film/television entrapment, who among us is willing to give up his radios, let alone his automobiles, in an attempt to return to a less alluring and less complicated era?

If these three basic items (movies, cars and radios), now so indelibly and deeply ingrained into our society, have been able to affect things so powerfully, what does the future hold in light of the technological advancements that are being proffered to us daily?

That technology adversely affected America's response to religious enthusiasm is obvious in its treatment of Billy Sunday's ministry. As obvious, is the fact that technology has greatly advanced our ability to spread the truth of the Gospel. *Even the most technologically careful among us* use machinery on a daily basis that was all but unimagined in Billy Sunday's day: computers, copiers, fax machines, calculators, radio advertisements, telephones and cell phones with world wide instant access, jet travel, and ultra comfortable automobiles, many of them with global positioning systems.

The questions of ***propriety*** in technology arises from its ability to allow the user access to things that are morally unclean, or appeal to the base, carnal nature of fallen man. Pornography of every vile sort, put forth by the peddlers of smut, to the very *sickest* of predators can also be found. These predators, like spiders weaving their web, hunt for people of like minds, as well as for the innocent and curious. Tales of ensnared children, addicted parents, broken homes and shattered lives abound, and this also is just getting started.

Answers to all of the questions now facing our entire society—let alone the people of God—are not easy to come by. While it is easy for someone to *say;* "Don't have *anything* to do with any of it," reality simply does not allow us that luxury (unless we want to go the route of the Amish peoples, and—believe me—they have their own special and select set of problems). If the Lord tarries, within a few years our children will be called upon to use these types of technology daily in *even the most menial* of public workplaces.

As a result, we are being pressed to find solutions to problems we never dreamed we would face. Just one example of the many dilemmas now facing our world is played out continually in the field of medical science. Thousand of families have been torn to pieces while trying to render judgments concerning 'life support systems.' One segment of a family may want to have a loved one's life 'supported' by such machinery in order to give God every chance to heal them. Another equally loving part of the family may be for removing the individual *off* the life support in order to give God His opportunity to heal or let the patient find his rest in peace. As a pastor I have had to intervene in physical altercations between anguished family members faced with these decisions. Furthermore I have witnessed both death, and healing of people whose families decided on opposite courses of action. Go figure.

Prior to the development of these modern life support systems, fateful decisions like this were *not even an option*. Nature alone decided the individual's span of life. Debates are now delving into areas of; parents having the right to clone a child that is surely about to pass away, or even transplanting the healthy head of a person whose body is dying onto the healthy body of a person who is brain dead. The individual would be paralyzed from the neck down but would still be alive, hence—theoretically at least—it would give the world a chance to have an ongoing mind around, such as Steven Hawking, or—had this been plausible earlier—Albert Einstein's. While we all appreciate the progress of medical science, moral dilemmas are being created that are frightening to contemplate.

Pet owners have for the past several years been able to have satellite traceable microchips placed into their animals in order to find them when lost or stolen. Hospitals are now considering using this chip to ensure that there are no mix-ups of babies, while parents contemplate the thought that knowing the location of their child is far more important than knowing where their dog is. Penal institutions are seriously considering the same for the incarcerated thus insuring the futility of escape attempts, especially prisoners who are criminally insane. Military uses for these chips abound. Not only would it give the immediate location of every soldier, these chips—already developed—have the ability to warm the body temperature through radio waves in case the soldier(s) are placed in freezing temperatures. They also have the ability through the same use of radio waves to destroy the recipients heart, or liver or kidneys—if the 'powers that be' are through with their services.

In the near future grocery shoppers will be able to fill their carts and simply walk through an instantaneous tunnel checkout straight to their car. Every item will be simultaneously read by its UPC bar code and the money withdrawn from their account or charged to their credit card. The stores inventory will be kept up to date instantly with orders for replacement goods becoming automatic. Advertisers as well as insurance companies will pay top dollar for the information concerning your spending and eating habits. As all cards have the ability to be reproduced, these transactions could be accomplished with far greater security and ease with a chip implant.

The thought of a cashless society grows more appetizing all the time to the governments of this world. This due to the robberies committed for cash, non-traceable cash drug deals, avoidance of paying taxes by under the table cash payments, as well as serious counterfeiting problems. Also, due to escalating credit card theft and fraud—a well placed—computer accessing—satellite spotting—business transacting microchip—placed into an individual would solve a host of problems.

Today, the number one factor for the expediency of this technology is due to the efforts to control terrorism. And until the recent tragedies brought about by terrorists, the personal freedoms of Americans have been valued above their personal safety. That has now been changed…forever.

Where is all of this leading? Those who know their eschatology know that ultimately it ends in the 'mark of the beast.'

"And he causeth all, both small and great, rich and poor, free and bond, to receive a mark in their right hand, or in their foreheads: And that no man might buy or sell, save he that had the mark, or the name of the beast, or the number of his name. Here is wisdom. Let him that hath understanding count the number of the beast: for it is the number of a man; and his number is Six hundred threescore and six." (Rev 13:16-14)

Again, are we to withdraw ourselves from society? Do we hew ourselves out communes in the wilderness, stock it with canned goods, dried fruit and firearms? Of course not. The words of Jesus are if anything more applicable now than ever... "Ye are the light of the world. A city that is set on an hill cannot be hid. Neither do men light a candle, and put it under a bushel, but on a candlestick; and it giveth light unto all that are in the house. Let your light so shine before men, that they may see your good works, and glorify your Father which is in heaven." (Matt 5:14-16)

The Church is ordained to be *the force of truth and revival* that hell has to reckon with in these last perilous days. At the same time the Church must feel its way prayerfully through all of the world's technological perils. Be the subject; medical science, personal home computers, internet, DVD, there are *no really easy* answers. But there is a faithful God who knows all, sees all and will see us through.

Society vs. Television

Few inventions have affected the world more than television. The avenues of its influence are so many and varied that to enumerate them here would require a chapter, yea a book of its own. Suffice it to say, as far as its moral effect on our world, it has been catastrophic. Almost without exception, that which is debased, vulgar, immoral, violent and blasphemous pours in a continual stream into the homes and hearts of American and world society. The long term result of the sowing of this hi-tech, slickly presented barrage of wickedness is readily seen, as the crop has now matured into an unstable and selfish society seemingly bent on destroying itself.

In a 1991 newspaper article entitled "The Death of Eloquence," Professor of Linguistics, Todd Gitlin of University of California, Berkeley stated that the average writing vocabulary of United States school children ages six to fourteen in 1945 was approximately 25,000 words. Forty-five years later in 1990, it had been reduced to less than 10,000 words. The number one culprit for a 60% loss of writing vocabulary was—television. Children who no longer read, but have the most common, base and limited vocabulary ran through their vulnerable minds like a freight train on a daily basis, cannot be expected to write and think with skills that previous generations had to master through diligence and self discipline.

Television and the Church

In about 1964, Pastor Paul Reynolds of British Columbia, Canada won an elderly Minister by the name of M. S. Winger to the Gospel from the largest trinity Pentecostal denomination in North America. Martin Winger fell in love with the New Birth message of Acts 2:38 and the Oneness of God and he was enthralled at the Holiness message that he found to be still alive in our movement. These truths he preached fervently until his death. One day as Brother Winger and Pastor Reynolds discussed the loss of the Holiness message in Brother Winger's former denomination, Brother Winger explained his view of what had happened.

Brother Winger was the District Superintendent of the New Brunswick District of the Assemblies of God of Canada when that movement officially declared that television was acceptable for their people to own and watch. When this took place Brother Winger resigned as Superintendent, being heartsick over what he knew to be a grievous error. Brother Winger stated that once the stand of allowing television had been officially implemented it took only about *one year's time* for the Assemblies as a movement to virtually cave in across the board on virtually every stand they had held through the years. In a very short time their women were wearing pants, jewelry, cosmetics and cutting their hair. Sad to say, a host of pastor's wives led the way. Things they had stood against since their earliest days as a movement, were now thrown overboard with abandon. It was as if a great on-rush of worldliness had been held in abeyance, and then, one day, 'the boy took his finger out of the dyke' and the whole world came sweeping in like a flood.

In much the same way, the Church of God of Cleveland, Tennessee took strong stands of separation from the world in many of its churches and officially in its Articles of Faith. As it is in our ranks, there were some areas of the country and certain 'districts' that were stronger than others on various issues, but, by and large, one could tell they were a Pentecostal movement that endeavored to live a godly lifestyle. Then in 1988 it all changed. At a General Conference held that year they voted to change their articles of faith concerning statements on separation from the world and modesty. Again, in just a short period of time, churches that once taught sanctity and holiness became ravaged with worldliness. In some of the larger churches where the women and girls previously adorned themselves in modest apparel as became women professing Godliness, they would now parade themselves across church platforms in bathing suits competing in beauty contests.

I pray to God, that our movement will not be swept away down stream in this torrent of carnality and worldliness, although, alas, large and ever growing segments are falling prey to it. If we fail to see the role that television has played in all of this we are guilty of willful ignorance.

***

Several years ago I listened to a powerful testimonial of Sister Ola Roeder about how God dealt with their family concerning television. During the writing of this book I called her to reaffirm the details of the story and get permission to print it. These events took place in Galien, Michigan in 1966 just after Sister Roeder came into the church.

She related that when she received the Holy Ghost and was baptized in Jesus Name, she was very quickly convicted of viewing television by a dream she had from the Lord. In the dream, she was walking down the streets of her rather small town at night. In every home she could see a dull bluish light coming from the windows. As she approached her home she saw she the same light coming from her own window. The Lord then spoke to her saying; "Come, I wish to show to you the god of the house." As she approached her home she noticed her family sitting on the couch and utterly intent upon the source of the light. As she could not see where the light was coming from she had to press her face to the far edge of the window in order to view "the god of the house." What she saw was a television. She awoke from the dream instantly and knew it was from the Lord.

When she told her husband about the dream he just laughed and said she was crazy. As she continued to talk about it and he continued to scoff, she said, "Look, if I pray that God blows up our television set would you believe it then?" He said; "Sure!" Sister Roeder then went across the room, placed her hands on top of the TV and prayed. "God, if that dream was from you, and this television is an idol in this house, I want you to ruin it right now!" Immediately a puff of smoke arose from the back of the TV and it could not be turned on.

Her husband looked astounded but said, "That was nothing but a coincidence." He took it the next day to a television repair shop and paid $44.00 to get it repaired. Remember that $44.00 back in 1966 was a lot more money than it is today. When he brought the TV back into their home, she could not believe it. After much discussion between them she finally said, "If I lay my hands on that thing and pray again that it blows up, would you then believe that it was God?" He affirmed that he would. She walked over to the TV, laid her hands on it and prayed the almost exact prayer as before. This time they heard a loud pop, and a very large cloud of smoke arose out from the television.

When Don Roeder took it back to the repair shop they told him that this time it was beyond repair. He bought a new one, but was later saved, rid his home of the television, entered the ministry and is now pastoring in Sawyer, Michigan.

My Testimony

I was not brought up in Church and was all but raised in front of the television. As I was born in 1952 I also watched Television "grow up" into what it is today. The programming of that day is a far cry from what it is today. Subjects such as sex that were vaguely alluded to back then are now brazenly thrown into the face of eager viewers. Everything from flirting to displayed homosexual liaisons is now standard fare for America. When it comes to God's standards of righteous life, there is not one sin named in the Bible, from Genesis to Revelation that is not openly depicted on television and that as an acceptable, tantalizing lifestyle.

How it Happened With Me

I was living in Denver Colorado in 1971 when the clock struck midnight on New Years Eve. I walked downstairs from a raucous party into a new year and towards a new life. As I lay upon my bed listening to the reveling upstairs I began to pray, repent and give my heart to God. I knew absolutely nothing about Pentecost and next to nothing about the Bible. All I knew was to tell God how sorry I was for the wretched life I had lived. That night I quit my smoking, all my drugs and everything else I intrinsically knew was wrong in the sight of God. It was but a few days later, after I had moved back to my parent's home in Pueblo and had started college, that God convicted me of watching television.

In my parent's home there is a television in almost every single room and it has been that way for years. A few nights after my repentance I was watching a program called "The Wild Wild West." Its hero, James West, had just beaten a man's head on a hitching post and tossed him into a watering trough. As I eagerly watched this, my heart suddenly grew very heavy and I said to myself; "James West… that was not a very Christian thing to do." I then changed the channel but quickly realized that what was on that station was not Christian. I went through a few more channels; realized the same, and finally turned it off and *never* went back to it. Please keep in mind I did not yet have or even know about the Holy Ghost, was not baptized in Jesus' Name, had no pastor, no church, and could quote only one verse (John 3:16) but could barely find it in the Bible.

It was not until fifteen years later, and I was pastoring in Arroyo Grande, California that I saw how beautiful the hand of God was upon me that night in Pueblo.

We had baptized a new couple, Ken and Laura Winkler, as they had received the Holy Ghost in their home. They had attended only a couple of our services. Ken and his wife were from a denominal church background and had always been hungry for more of God. One night at the close of prayer meeting, he approached and asked if he could ask me a few questions. I assured him he could and he proceeded to say; "If you don't mind I'd like you to tell me everything that this church teaches concerning separation from the world and modesty. Tell me what all of the church 'rules' are."

As this is not something that happens every day I was a little taken aback and told him that if he would just stick around, through preaching, teaching, praying, observation and asking questions, it would all come to him in the process of time. He replied that he and his wife would just as soon know now and really get started right. Any Pastor knows that this can be a wonderful moment or something that can backfire in your face. As Ken continued to insist I picked up a Bible and began to walk him through 'the lines and precepts' of our most basic stands of modesty and separation from ungodliness. Throughout this process he would ask a question here and there, but basically saw and understood everything.

When I came to the subject of television he said; "Oh that's no problem whatsoever... we haven't owned a TV for six years." I was taken aback and asked him 'why,' as I knew the church he had been in had never spoken out against any worldliness much less television. Ken said; "Oh I know, in fact people in that church would make fun of us for not having a television. But six years ago I was watching an old TV show called the Wild Wild West, and this guy named James West had just beaten a man's head on a hitching post and thrown him into a watering trough. It was then that I thought, 'You know, that was not the Christian thing to do.' I got convicted from that moment, got rid of my television and we never watched it again." I could not believe what I was hearing but raised my hands and began to thank the Lord for His wonderful works to the children of men.

Ken went on to tell me how that when he was in the Navy, he had to serve a six month stretch on a U.S. nuclear submarine. During that time—of no doubt extreme boredom—he only *one time* slipped in to watch a Walt Disney movie—got convicted after just a few minutes and got up and left. When I think of the 'lack of conviction' found in many pastors and people of our churches today—who are supposed to have the Holy Ghost—I cringe. Today Ken and his wife are in the ministry and have raised a beautiful, talented family for the Lord.

David's Psalm and Moses injunction are still viable for us today.

"I will behave myself wisely in a perfect way. O when wilt thou come unto me? **I will walk within my house with a perfect heart. I will set no wicked thing before mine eyes: I hate the work of them that turn aside; it shall not cleave to me.**" (Psalms 101:2)

"Neither shalt thou bring an abomination **into thine house, lest** thou be a **cursed thing like it:** but thou shalt utterly detest it, and thou shalt utterly abhor it; for it is a cursed thing." (Deuteronomy 7:26)

Video and the Stumbling Block

A ministerial associate first introduced me to VCR technology in the early 1980's. My first glimpse of it was when we were walking together through a shopping mall. As he spoke to me of the possibilities of it being used as a teaching tool for Pastors, aspiring ministers, saints, young people, missionaries and for reaching the lost, I was very much impressed with its possibilities (albeit I did not buy one). As the next few years began to unfold it began to come to my attention that while saints and ministers alike were using it, it was also being utilized for almost everything other than that for which they had originally intended. Hollywood productions of all types were being viewed and many times by people who had been held in high esteem for their stands against those very things. The more I heard, the more distressed I became as I realized that righteous stands taken years before by our movement against Hollywood and Television were slowly—in many cases not so slowly—being undermined.

Before long whole congregations were feeding from the trough of the world through the medium of the Video Cassette Recorder. It seemed that when once purchased, it was but a relatively short period of time before viewing materials went from church services and grandchildren to 'educational documentaries' to movies or cartoons of at first 'marginal' propriety, but were being quickly replaced by movies that were without question *not* what God intended for His people to partake of. John and James were surely used of God when they wrote:

"Love not the world, neither the things that are in the world. If any man love the world, the love of the Father is not in him." (1 John 2:15)

"Ye adulterers and adulteresses, know ye not that the friendship of the world is enmity with God? Whosoever therefore will be a friend of the world is the enemy of God.

Do ye think that the scripture saith in vain, the spirit that dwelleth in us lusteth to envy?" (James 4:4-5)

"Or what do you think the Scripture means when it says that the Holy Spirit, whom God has placed within us, watches over us with tender jealousy?" (Tay)

I finally came to the place that while I understood that video technology did have possibilities for good, far too many of God's people using it were stumbling into areas that they never dreamed they would go. This is tragic but not surprising when you consider what the preacher said in Ecclesiastes 1:8 "...The eye is not satisfied with seeing, nor the ear filled with hearing."

I once discussed these concerns with a pastor who had watched a movie based on a book that I had read. When he asked me what the difference was between me reading the book and him watching the movie, I answered, "Ten years. You keep watching movies and I'll stick to reading books and in ten years we'll see where each of us are." That was in 1984 and almost twenty years have passed. I am very happy to relate that this man caught himself, does not now watch any movies nor own a VCR, and does not have them in his church. But there were others that day within earshot of our conversation that did not catch themselves and who have suffered very detrimentally spiritually. Some of them are no longer even in the faith.

Without question, far more Christians are going to be lost over 'Hollywood' type entertainments than are ever going to be saved in spite of them.

Stumbling Blocks

Several years ago a man came to God in our church who worked at a local nuclear power plant. Through process of time he informed me that he was quite a hunter but did not use firearms. He would carefully work his way through the woods with his Video Cassette Recorder and take footage of wild life. Basically, that was all he used it for. Very rarely, before he came to God, had he used it to watch any 'Hollywood' production and certainly did not do so now.

There was no way that I could tell him that his filming of forest creatures was in any way harmful to him or anyone else. It was obviously a fulfilling and mentally relaxing pastime that any thoughtful individual could appreciate. What I did point out however, was that while his use of this technology as his hobby was beyond reproach, not everyone had the ability to handle it as well as he. It was my sad duty to inform him that other people in the church could not control VCR but rather, in moments of weakness, found themselves pulled inexorably into the Hollywood trap, delving ever deeper into worse and worse materials. They simply could not handle it and were overcame by it. For this reason I asked our people to please not have a VCR in their homes, lest they be a stumbling block to themselves, their families and to other saints that could trip up over their use of it—however proper. One portion of scripture that I directed him to was Romans 14:14-16;

"I know, and am persuaded by the Lord Jesus, that there is nothing unclean of itself: but to him that esteemeth any thing to be unclean, to him it is unclean. But if thy brother be grieved with thy meat, now walkest thou not charitably. Destroy not him with thy meat, for whom Christ died. Let not then your good be evil spoken of."

This plea was made to him and our church in the latter 1980's. I am gratified to say that he not only complied but also thoroughly understood where I as a pastor was coming from—and never looked back.

**

A couple of years later a very good man in our church called me and asked if I could possibly come over to his house within the next few days as he had something he wanted to show me. I said I would, but was actually not able to make it there for about two weeks. When I called and said I finally could come, he asked for me to drop in the next evening as he had returned the items he wished to show me.

When I arrived at his home he turned on his computer, inserted a 'CD-Rom' (which was a new innovation to me at that time) pushed some buttons and lo—I began seeing commercials that were obviously made for television. This brother (who made his living by keeping the computer system for a major University in repair) then patiently explained to me that CD-Rom was just the beginning in a new wave of future technology—which I immediately saw was no doubt true. When he asked me, "What we were going to do about it?"… I sat there for a long, long time before finally looking up at him and saying, "You know Steve…the time has come that circumcision *really is going to have to begin at the heart*." I made that statement almost fifteen years ago, and I have seen nothing since to change my mind.

As a pastor, it was not very long before I understood that—no matter how far to the right I made my stand, I was being outflanked by yet better (or worse) computer technology. I dare say, there is not one conscientious pastor that has not been deeply troubled as to just exactly what they should do in these matters. For one thing, *it is here to stay*, and for another, it is daily becoming more streamlined and accessible. The youngest child in grade school is being taught computer literacy, as educators know that the future workplace is going to demand it, *in even the most menial positions*. The church of God is not going to be able to cross its fingers, close its eyes and 'wish it away.' We are rather being forced to come to a place of consecration and spiritual maturity that we not be destroyed spiritually as people of God. For without doubt we *will* find ourselves and *especially* our children using it in years if not days to come.

***

In all fairness, when discussing 'stumbling blocks' we must keep in mind that an 'erring heart' can stumble over just about anything that makes it convenient to do so. As a case in point, I remember receiving a phone call several years ago from a young man who had graduated from our Christian school. Though never a member of our church, he was a nice young man that we all very much liked. He called me and in tears stated that his father had just 'thrown him out' of his home. I knew his father fairly well and as he was very much a gentleman, could not imagine what had happened. I said "Tim (not his real name) what have you done?"

"Well" he said, "I had been making some phone calls that I shouldn't have."

"Tim, what kind of calls?"

"Well…I've been making some calls to 900 numbers."

My heart sank, and I said, "Oh Tim… do you mean calls where you talk to women?"

"Yes sir" he said, his voice getting quieter all the time.

"Tim," I said, "How long have you been doing this?"

"Only about three... or four weeks, sir."

"Did the phone bill come in?"

"Yes, sir. That's how my dad found out, and that's why he's thrown me out."

"How much was the bill, Tim?"

"Six thousand, two hundred dollars."

I now understood his father's shock and anger. It was also at that moment that it really dawned on me that if an individual has a mind to get into mischief, our world has made it exceedingly easy to do so. One could say that his father having a phone in the home was a stumblingblock to his son, but how well would any of us function without telephones (though, no doubt, we are often tempted to try).

Nevertheless, a Conscientious Effort Must be Made...

"Wherefore seeing we also are compassed about with so great a cloud of witnesses, let us **lay aside every weight, and the sin which doth so easily beset us**, and let us run with patience the race that is set before us, looking unto Jesus the author and finisher of our faith; who for the joy that was set before him endured the cross, despising the shame, and is set down at the right hand of the throne of God. For consider him that endured such contradiction of sinners against himself, **lest ye be wearied and faint in your minds.**" (Hebrews 12:1-3)

"Finally, brethren, whatsoever things are **true**, whatsoever things are **honest**, whatsoever things are **just**, whatsoever things are **pure**, whatsoever things are **lovely**, whatsoever things are of **good report**;

if there be **any virtue**, and if there be **any praise**, *think on these things*." (Philippians 4:8)

God indeed honors the efforts made by conscientious pastors who labor to keep sin and the world out of the church. Surely there is a special place in Heaven for such people. When one considers that the minister stands against an entire world system, every demon Hell can throw against him, just enough carnal saints to keep him on his knees—and his own human nature, it is amazing that any man can still set his face and keep on preaching and teaching against the evils of this present age. Paul no doubt said it best;

"...and who is sufficient for these things?" (2 Cor. 2:16)

"…and who is equal to such a task?" (NIV)

"…and who is adequate for these things?" (NASB)

But God in His wisdom chose it to be this way, and has provided the needed grace;

"And he said unto me, My grace is sufficient for thee: for my strength is made perfect in weakness." (2 Cor. 12:9)

And that God chose for his ministry, human beings that have to 'wage war in themselves' also is clearly seen in Hebrews 5:1-2;

"For every high priest taken **from among men** is ordained for men in things pertaining to God, that he may offer both gifts and sacrifices for sins: **Who can have compassion** on the ignorant, and on them that are out of the way; **for that he himself also is compassed with infirmity.**"

The Internet

Probably the number one item of concern—at least at this juncture in time is—the Internet. An attempt to describe its pro's and con's in any semblance of detail is unrealistic, as the Internet is so big, covers so many areas, and growing so fast as to be well nigh impossible to keep up with. Suffice it to say, the key word is *ACCESS*. The Internet gives access to almost every type of knowledge that is available in the world today. There are few if any subjects that are not covered by it, and as far as what the future holds, it is in its infancy stage. In-depth information abounds in every field of history, mathematics, theology, sociology, psychology, health care, literature, music, science, etc. etc. etc. Information can be found concerning nations, cities, companies, families, individuals… the list is absolutely endless, and growing every day. Again, this has unbelievable potential for both good and evil and without question is being used for both.

What are We to Do?

Many safeguards to the dangers of Internet have been suggested not just by our people, but by other religious as well as secular individuals who have genuine concerns over the moral, spiritual and emotional dangers with which it is fraught.

First, let me say that while I have not personally banned it from either my home or congregation, *I have no problem whatsoever with those that do.* They no doubt are taking the safest route possible and I would never argue with that. At the same time, I am not completely sure as to any church's long-term ability to be able to keep that stand.

More and more companies are encouraging, and in some cases demanding, that certain amounts of the workload be accomplished in the homes of their employees. Many individuals who have their own businesses must, of necessity, do at least part of their work from the home. To a very great degree, the number one form of communication in all of this is e-mail, a use which will only increase until its use soon surpasses even the telephone. Computer communication for business transaction is even more attractive now that air travel has been so deeply affected by the threat of terrorism.

The following are some of the steps that I personally know that pastors and families have taken in order to protect their homes against the abuse and corruption available on the Internet.

1. DO NOT USE IT AT ALL ANYWHERE OR AT ANY-TIME.

2. USE IT ONLY AT THE PLACE OF BUSINESS OUTSIDE OF THE HOME.

3. IF USED AT HOME, IT MUST BE USED FOR BUSINESS PURPOSES ONLY, NOTHING ELSE—NOT EVEN FOR EDUCATION.

4. IF USED AT HOME, USE IT ONLY FOR BUSINESS *AND* EDUCATION

5. IF USED AT HOME, MUST HAVE AN ONLINE FILTER SERVICE OR INTERNAL FILTER OR BOTH.

6. IF USED AT HOME, IT MUST BE SET IN THE FRONT ROOM OR FAMILY ROOM WHERE PEOPLE CON-GREGATE, THAT IT NOT BE IN SECRET, WHERE IT COULD BECOME TO GREAT A TEMPTATION TO VISIT RESTRICTED, UNHEALTHY, UNSAFE WEB SITES

While I have no problem with any of these recommendations, I personally feel that the first one is in reality, impractical. Not that it cannot be done of course, (I personally do not even know how to get on it, or even how to send or receive email) but by the time a church begins to grow to any size, and pulls in a cross section of people from different backgrounds, it will be unlikely for there not to be *someone* who must genuinely utilize the internet at least in the workplace. For my family and the church that I pastor, I require that at the bare minimum an "X-Block" be installed that blocks out any words of pornographic nature.

Shadrach, Meshach and Abednego

In the opening paragraph of this chapter the remark was made that; "Every God fearing pastor and saint is going to have to work out for themselves what devices should be allowed in the home or workplace." The reason for that statement is that technology has brought this principle into an extremely sharp focus. The saints of God are themselves going to have to develop deep convictions as to what is right and wrong, acceptable and unacceptable in the sight of God, and live thereby.

In the third chapter of the book of Daniel, we read of the golden image erected by King Nebuchadnezzar. He commanded that all in his domain bow down and worship the image once they began to hear; "...the sound of the cornet, flute, harp, sackbut, psaltery, dulcimer, and all kinds of musick." (Chapter 3:5) To those children of Israel who had already compromised themselves by the eating of the king's meat and drinking king's wine which had been offered to the king's gods, it was but one more simple step to now fall down and worship this image. In doing so they were breaking both the first and second of the Ten Commandments given them at Sinai.

"Thou shalt have no other gods before me."

"Thou shalt not make unto thee any graven image, or any likeness of any thing that is in heaven above, or that is in the earth beneath, or that is in the water under the earth: Thou shalt not bow down thyself to them, nor serve them..." (Ex 20:3-5)

Three Hebrews however refused to bow down before Nebuchadnezzor's idol. The three Hebrew children, that along with Daniel purposed in their hearts not to defile themselves, once again resolved to do the same.

Where was Daniel?

The question that begs to be asked is "Where was Daniel in all of this?" I feel that I received the answer to that several years ago. Daniel was…wherever God wanted him to be. On that particular occasion, God did not want him *there*. God desired to see what Shadrach, Meshach and Abednego would do without being in the presence of their 'pastor.'

It is one thing for leadership to purpose in their heart not to be defiled, but it is another for those that follow to do the same.

"Then Nebuchadnezzar in his rage and fury commanded to bring Shadrach, Meshach, and Abed-nego. Then they brought these men before the king. Nebuchadnezzar spake and said unto them, Is it true, O Shadrach, Meshach, and Abed-nego, do not ye serve my gods, nor worship the golden image which I have set up?" (Dan 3:13-14)

"Shadrach, Meshach, and Abednego, answered and said to the king, O Nebuchadnezzar, we are **not careful** to answer thee in this matter. If it be so, our God whom we serve is able to deliver us from the burning fiery furnace, and he will deliver us out of thine hand, O king. But if not, be it known unto thee, O king, that we will not serve thy gods, nor worship the golden image which thou hast set up." (Verses 16-18)

Here again, I make the statement; 'Every God fearing pastor *and saint* is going to have to work out for themselves what devices should be allowed in the home or workplace.' In light of the advancements of modern technology the time has come for all saints, young and old, children or parents to receive and embrace deep convictions against the ungodliness that permeates this world, regardless of where it is found and in what medium.

We Must Draw a Line...
and What a Difference a Line Can Make

"For the wrath of God is revealed from heaven against all ungodliness and unrighteousness of men, who hold the truth in unrighteousness" (Rom 1:18)

"And even as they did not like to retain God in their knowledge, God gave them over to a reprobate mind, to do those things which are not convenient; Being filled with all unrighteousness, fornication, wickedness, covetousness, maliciousness; full of envy, murder, debate, deceit, malignity; whisperers, Backbiters, haters of God, despiteful, proud, boasters, inventors of evil things, disobedient to parents, Without understanding, covenantbreakers, without natural affection, implacable, unmerciful: Who knowing the judgment of God, that they which commit such things are worthy of death, not only do the same, **but have pleasure in them that do them**." (Rom 1:28-31)

The overriding theme of the Hollywood film/Television industry is that *everything* that God is against...it is unabashedly for. Be it; unrighteousness, fornication, wickedness, covetousness, maliciousness, envy, murder, debate, deceit, malignity, backbiting, God hating, despising, pride, boasting, creating of evil things, disobedience to parents, promise breaking, unnatural affection, having ruthlessness." Not only does the entertainment industry promote these things but does so by putting them in the best possible light while portraying all that is godly, righteous and biblical as being absurdly foolish.

For a Christian to look to sin for entertainment is a very grievous error. For them to excuse this by their non-involvement in the actions taking place is inexcusable.

"Who knowing the judgment of God, that they which commit such things are worthy of death, not only do the same, but **have pleasure in them that do them**." (Rom 1:32)

"Although they know God's righteous decree that those who do such things deserve death, they not only continue to do these very things but also **approve of those who practice them.** (Rom 1:32 NIV)

***

The theme of this book is, "What a difference a line can make." When it comes to modern technology, people are of necessity going to have to draw the proper lines in their heart and keep them. As Daniel '*purposed in his heart not to defile himself*' so we must do the same, individually and collectively. Every saint of God must rise up with their pastor and take proper stands for righteousness that help create the climate and atmosphere where holiness and grace abound and spirituality can flourish. *No pastor can do it alone—nor should he have to.*

Chapter Eleven

Sports, the god of this World

merica has 'gone to seed' over sports. From the amount of space and time that it receives in the media to the astronomical salaries that its stars receive, one must readily concede that sports is one of America's most lucrative, riveting, and aggressive businesses. Children from their earliest years are harried to produce on the playing fields of baseball, football, basketball and soccer. Overzealous parents and coaches place unbelievable pressure upon these children to perform. Many psychologists (not just Pentecostal ministers) are warning of the negatives of pressured involvement in competitive sports.

Without dissecting the most salient points, I would like to briefly note some items concerning sports that without question reveal the absurdly high value that is placed on something of such a low nature.

1. The unbelievably, outrageously high salaries paid to these court gladiators (absolutely no one receives 8.5 million dollars per year to merely "play a game").
2. The reality of the very negative lifestyles of many of these 'heroes' and 'icons' of the world's youth. A case in point being that the NBA revealed that 357 of its players had fathered 357 illegitimate children. One 'star' has sired 10 out of wedlock babies.
3. College and Professional sports have become 'hotbeds' of betting and gambling.
4. Its addictive power to be seen in the unbelievable sums

that advertisers pay Network Television for time spots and the vast audiences that are glued into the games.

5. It has been duly noted that some Oneness churches actually dismiss their service on 'Super Bowl Sunday' in order that no one miss the game. One church I know brought a wide screen television into their fellowship hall for the church to gather around, popcorn and drink in hand. *God help us all.*

6. In its totality the entire system of the organized sports world is based on carnality without a glimmer of spirituality unless you count a pre-game prayer for God to cause one of the teams to be the victor—while God no doubt could frankly care less.

My Experience

Several years ago a man that I was attempting to pastor, informed me that he had joined a bowling team, would be involved in tournaments, and that unless I could prove to him in scripture that it was wrong, was not about to quit. To say that this man was not the most spiritual individual I have ever pastored is an understatement. It was my first pastorate, I was several years younger than he and had been working hard at being his pastor for about a year. We had only recently been able to convince him—for the sake of his children if nothing else—to rid his home of television.

In my attempt to convince him that this was not a good direction for him to go, I began to show him scriptures that I had been taught concerning the dangers of becoming entangled in sports in anything beyond an occasional, and certainly loose nit involvement.

"No man that warreth **entangleth himself** with the affairs of this life; that he may please him who hath chosen him to be a soldier." (2 Timothy 2:4)

"...I hate the work of them that **turn aside**; it shall **not cleave to me**." (Psalms 101:3)

"So then they that are **in the flesh** cannot please God." (Romans 8:8)

He was not impressed, said those scriptures were not good enough for him, and was going ahead with his plans and his team. Being a very young and as yet inexperienced pastor, this 'shook me' as I could not believe his intransigence. I wondered if I was being too exacting in telling him that his decision would not be pleasing to God and began to *earnestly* seek God over the matter. I asked God to personally reveal to me what His feelings were about this matter of 'organized sports.' While I believed those things my Pastor taught me, I wanted desperately to hear from God for myself and to know exactly how He felt.

For two weeks I sought God fervently and daily concerning this situation. One evening, after speaking in a service in Oklahoma City, and resting in a recliner in the Pastor's office, the Lord gave me my answer. The following scriptures began pouring through my heart and I felt completely assured that God had revealed to me his feelings about His people becoming entangled in anything which possesses the power to swerve us from our utmost devotion and service to Him. What was given was a precept concerning our allegiance and devotion to Him. What follows is what I received from the Lord.

***

Through a host of scriptures we understand that marriage is an institution created and blessed of God. It is obviously His will that marriages take place and His desire is to bless the unions and the ensuing families. The following are just a few of these scriptures.

"And the LORD God said, it is not good that the man should be alone; I will make him an help meet for him." (Genesis 2:18)

"Whoso findeth a wife findeth a good thing, and obtaineth favour of the LORD." (Proverbs 18:22)

"As arrows are in the hand of a mighty man; so are children of the youth. Happy is the man that hath his quiver full of them…" (Psalms 127:4-5)

"Marriage is honourable in all, and the bed undefiled: but whoremongers and adulterers God will judge." (Hebrews 13:4)

However, in Paul's first letter to the Corinthian Church, he allows that even an institution ordained of God and as hallowed as marriage, has the potential to distract one from giving God their very best service.

"But this I say, brethren, the time is short: it remaineth, that both they that **have wives** be as though they had none; And they that weep, as though they wept not; and they that rejoice, as though they rejoiced not; and they that buy, as though they possessed not; And they that use this world, as not abusing it: for the fashion of this world passeth away. But I would have you without carefulness. He that **is unmarried careth for the things that belong to the Lord, how he may please the Lord: But he that is married careth for the things that are of the world, how he may please his wife.** There is difference also between a wife and a virgin. The **unmarried woman careth for the things of the Lord, that she may be holy both in body and in spirit: but she that is married careth for the things of the world, how she may please her husband.**" (1 Cor. 7:29-34)

PLEASE NOTE VERSE 35:

"And this I speak for your own profit; not that I may **cast a snare upon you**, but for that which is comely, and that ye **may attend upon the Lord without distraction.**"

"I am saying this for your own good, **not to restrict you**, but that you may **live in a right way in undivided devotion to the Lord.**" (NIV)

"This I say for your own benefit; **not to put a restraint upon you,** but to promote what is **appropriate and to secure undistracted devotion** to the Lord." (New American Standard)

"I am saying this to help you, **not to try to keep you from marrying.** I want you to do whatever will **help you serve the Lord best, with as few other things as possible to distract your attention from him.**" (Tay)

The apostle is not teaching against marriage, but instructing that *even an institution created and blessed by God* has the power, if we are not very careful to distract us away from our most directed and devoted service toward Him. If this is true of an institution as holy as marriage, *how much more should we beware of binding involvements into institutions which God has nothing to do with and are certainly not recipients of His blessing?* Such as sports teams of any type that require set practices and or games that could be held in cross-purposes of church services and activities. Add then, the demands made upon God's time, along with the emotional and even physical energy that God intends Himself to be the number one recipient of, and you see rather quickly that it is impossible to serve the one without being distracted from the other. Matt 6:24 still states it best;

"No man can serve two masters: for either he will hate the one, and love the other; or else he will hold to the one, and despise the other." He goes on to say that; *"Ye cannot serve God and mammon."* If I may interpolate; *"Ye also cannot serve God and sports"* or, *"God and secret societies,"* or anything of that nature. He is still "a jealous God," as Exodus 20:5-6 states; "Thou shalt not bow down thyself to them, [idols] nor serve them: for I the LORD thy God am a jealous God, visiting the iniquity of the fathers upon the children unto the third and fourth generation of them that hate me; (6) And shewing mercy unto thousands of them that love me, and keep my commandments.

I wish I could tell you that this man readily received this revelation, gave up his bowling team and lived happily ever after. Alas he still refused to listen, and as his self-will grew and spilled over into other areas, he and his entire family eventually lost out with God.

***

Twenty years later I found myself pastoring a young man who was being actively recruited by the football coaches at his high school. He came to me asking if I thought it would be all right if he joined the team. I placed my hands on his shoulders, looked into his eyes as kindly as I could and said;

"Son, the thing that really bothers me is that you are not coming to me asking what you can do to get closer to God, be more effective for the kingdom, or become more involved in winning the lost. What you are really saying is; 'How far out can I go in being entangled in this world and their gods and still keep one foot in church?' You're not asking; How close can I get to God? but, How far away can I get and still have Him?"

I am very gratified to say that this young man was of a different heart and spirit. He readily took my counsel, pressed in yet closer to God, said 'No' to the coaches, graduated and today is happily married, living for God and raising his family in Jesus Christ.

A Convicted Coach

A good fellow-pastor friend of mine related the following story years ago when he was a young man in high school, the basketball coach was ever goading him to join the team. My friend never came right out and said that he had a conviction against joining the basketball team or anything else that would bring him into cross-purposes with God, His Church commitments or modest dress standards. He would just kind of shuffle the toe of his shoe in the ground and say he didn't think he could do it.

Day after day the coach would 'rag' at him sometimes even in front of the class. Finally after several weeks of this, the coach asked him to stay after school so that he could talk to him.

The coach looked my friend in the eye and said; "Its your church isn't it? Your church doesn't believe in organized sports do they?"

My friend with his head down said; "No sir, they don't."

The coach said; "You are Pentecostal aren't you?"

"Yes sir" he said.

"Well Mike" the coach said, "Let me tell you something. Twenty-five years ago I was in your shoes. I was in church, and I was very good at sports. The difference was I joined the team, and as one thing led to another I drifted completely away from God, and as yet have never gone back. To be honest with you I'm not even sure I could make it back if I wanted to. Mike, what you are doing is right. Don't join this or any team. I was just checking you out, and really I am very sorry for what I've put you through. I'll never do it again."

Mike went on to become a pastor with a God given conviction against becoming involved with organized sports.

The Dream and Testimony of my Friend

Several years ago a good friend of mine took the pastorate of an old established church. He was in his mid-twenties and this was his first church. He was not there very long before he found out that four families in the church had their children involved in high school sports. As he was 'the new kid on the block,' very young, pretty much inexperienced and this was an old 'seasoned' church, he decided to move slowly and 'feel out the waters.'

The city he lived in was a small southern town and the High School sports activities were a big part of the social scene. In an effort to be objective he one night visited a high school football game. There was no drunkenness, relatively little cursing, good-natured rivalry and seemed to be a family type activity for the community. He came away thinking that maybe it was not as bad as he had thought and had been taught.

Football season passed into basketball season and then into the baseball season and as far as he could tell the same scenario of community camaraderie held true. He had just about decided against taking a stand against his young people's involvement when he had a series of three dreams.

The first night this young pastor and father dreamed the he and his only son were hunting. As they were making their way through a wooded area he and his seven-year old son were looking at each other, when this young pastor raised his shotgun and blew his horrified son to pieces. The pastor woke with a shriek and was shaking and covered with sweat.

The next night he dreamed that he and his son were driving in his car down a highway. As they were moving this young pastor reached over his sons lap, opened the car door and with his right leg began kicking the boy out the door. The utter terror on the face of the child was awful to behold. When the boy fell from the car, his dad could see him bouncing and rolling on the pavement in his rear view mirror. He then stopped the car put it in reverse and drove the car back over his son. Though it was a dream he could feel his body crunch under the wheels as he drove over him. The pastor again woke with a shriek, fell out of bed onto the floor and began crying asking God what in the world was going on.

The third night he dreamed yet again. This time he and the boy were standing by the side of the family swimming pool. Though the boy could not swim at that time the young pastor picked him up and threw him into the water. Somehow the boy, scrambling, splashing and gulping, made it to the side of the pool and grasped the ledge where his father stood. Then his father placed the heel of his shoe on his son's fingers and began to grind and crush them until the boy let go screaming, sliding below the surface of the water. He flailed his way back and again grabbed for the edge of the pool simply to have his dad crush his fingers again. As he slid below the surface of the water he looked into his father's face as if he was saying to him; "Why Dad... why did you do this to me?"

The young Pastor awoke and hit the floor sobbing saying "God... God what is wrong with me? What are you trying to tell me? Are you telling me that I am going to kill my son?"

This time the Lord spoke to him. "I am showing you what you are doing to my young people by allowing them to be involved in sports... you are killing them!" At this point, this young pastor and one of my good friends wept his way through to a firm stand that has held now for almost twenty years.

He called in the four families whose children were involved with High School sports, told them of his dreams and asked them to please quit. Two of the families did so immediately and all are living for God today. The other two families refused to comply, as they did not believe that the dreams nor the interpretation were from God. None of those family members are today living for God.

You will never be able to convince me that God is not concerned about our allegiances. As the Second of the Ten Commandments still teaches, God is a jealous God, loves us and knows what is best for us. It is this commandment that James refers to in his writings.

"Ye adulterers and adulteresses, know ye not that the friendship of the world is enmity with God? whosoever therefore will be a friend of the world is the enemy of God. Do ye think that the scripture saith in vain, The spirit that dwelleth in us lusteth to envy?" James 4:4-5 (KJV)

"Or what do you think the Scripture means when it says that the Holy Spirit, whom God has placed within us, **watches over us with tender jealousy?**" (Tay)

"You adulterous people, don't you know that **friendship with the world is hatred toward God? Anyone who chooses to be a friend of the world becomes an enemy of God.** Or do you think Scripture says without reason that **the spirit he caused to live in us envies intensely?**" (NIV)

This World as Honey

I read of a Honey merchant in India that would sell a ladle of honey onto small paper plates as a confectionary. Not being in an extremely clean environment, the flies would gather around honeyed plates and land as they could. The merchant would whisk them away with his hand and keep on selling. Upon chasing away the flies from his latest sale, he found that one fly had imbedded himself into the honey and could not free himself with the flick of a hand. The fly was removed by the proprietors fingers, squashed and the honey sold and eaten. The owner of the honey business still holding the dead fly said; "These flies are like people and this honey is like the things of this world. God does not mind His people enjoying this world—to a point, but He expects us not to get so involved that we cannot extract ourselves at a moments notice. This fly, (holding the squashed bug) is like some people who get in too deep and cannot free themselves and are thus destroyed."

The Apostle Paul put it in much the same way when he wrote; "All things are lawful unto me, but all things are not expedient: all things are lawful for me, *but I will not be brought under the power of any.* (1 Corinthians 6:12)

While we know that there is nothing wrong with playing a game of sports, be it football, basketball, baseball or hop scotch, we as saints of God should not be brought under its power as has our nation and world.

Chapter Twelve

Can You Throw Jezebel Out the Window?

"**B**ut there was none like unto Ahab, which did sell himself to work wickedness in the sight of the LORD, whom Jezebel his wife stirred up." (1 Kings 21:25)

As we come to the conclusion of this book concerning the vast differences that a single line, decision or stand can make, I am reminded of the story of the death of Jezebel at the hands of Jehu.

"And when Jehu was come to Jezreel, Jezebel heard of it; and she painted her face, and tired her head, and looked out at a window. And as Jehu entered in at the gate, she said, Had Zimri peace, who slew his master? And he lifted up his face to the window, and said, Who is on my side? Who? And there looked out to him two or three eunuchs. And he said, Throw her down. So they threw her down: and some of her blood was sprinkled on the wall, and on the horses: and he trode her under foot." (2 Kings 9:30-33)

After several years of a pitiless and debauched lifestyle, judgment had finally come to Ahab's house. As King Ahab, had already been slain in battle by a Syrian arrow "drawn at a venture," it was now Jezebel's turn to taste the violence and cruelty she had meted out over the years. Jehu, the newly anointed King, had entered Jezreel to finish the business of God's judgment.

One must hand it to Jezebel that her life, however wretched, was consistent to the end as she one more time paints her face, even in the face of judgment. Whether she was trying in a last ditch effort to entice Jehu by her wiles, or she simply had been into facial make-up so long that she could not bear the thought of being seen without it—even at her funeral—we do not know. Whatever the case, she is to the last, the same wanton, idolatrous, murderous woman that helped 'stir up' Ahab in bringing about the total ruination of Israel.

As she stands in her upper window, Jezebel gives Jehu a short but insightful history lesson on the cost of monarchal overthrow. Jehu is not particularly interested as he—at this time at least—is on an anointed mission from God. So he yells the question up to her house, "Who is on my side? Who?" The telling point of this rather gruesome affair is that it took *eunuchs* to get the job done. "And there looked out to him two or three eunuchs. And he said, Throw her down. So they threw her down…"

Due to their physical condition, Jezebel's seductive ways held absolutely no enticement for them. At the risk of sounding unfeelingly crude, to these eunuchs, throwing the wanton Jezebel out the window was as easy as throwing out a sack of rotting potatoes. She held no allure for them—she had no affect on them—they had no pull or attraction toward her because…they were eunuchs.

Eunuchs… for the Kingdoms Sake

"For there are some eunuchs, which were so born from their mother's womb: and there are some eunuchs, which were made eunuchs of men: and there be eunuchs, which have made themselves **eunuchs for the kingdom of heaven's sake**…" (Matt 19:12)

Though this verse concerns the will of God in marriage for certain individuals, nevertheless a strong inference can be made about the magnetism of the world upon people who have not sold out themselves completely to the will of God. Again, the men—the eunuchs—God used to throw Jezebel out the window had no trouble doing so as she held no appeal, no attraction, no fascination for them.

Could it be that the reason some preachers have a hard time drawing a line against television—throwing it out the window—is because the pull of it is too strong upon them as they have watched too much of it in their motel rooms.

They have a hard time taking a stand against Hollywood style productions, be they viewed in the Movie house, television, Video Cassete Recorders or DVDs, as they are readily viewed in the parsonage.

Church members are allowed to be swallowed up into the world of competitive sports due to the pastors (or his children's) addiction to it.

Preaching against the pornography that can be found on Internet is never mentioned due to their own involvement.

Dress standards for men and especially women are lacking decent direction due to their own desires for less than what is wholesome.

Pastors find it difficult to teach Paul's injunctions concerning men and women's hair because their wife has too big a pull in the other direction.

Facial hair on men is never discussed because of certain tithe payers who want it.

Jewelry has become a non-issue for the same reason… or maybe because their daughter or son wants a "class ring" or wife wants a wedding ring. [My intention here is not to offend or be hurtful—as I have good friends who allow wedding rings… *supposedly the only piece of jewelry allowed.* I am nevertheless of the tribe of 'no wedding rings.' To me this is more than just a personal conviction—the scriptures warrant the stand.]

Nevertheless;

It means something *to be able* to throw
'Jezebel' out the window!

The World vs. The Advocate

I have now been in the ministry for over thirty years, and have spent over twenty of it pastoring. During that time I have witnessed many successes and sadly, many failures. The statement that I am about to make—I ask the reader to consider carefully.

I have personally come to the place, that *if I had to choose*, between pastoring someone that failed God by 'falling into sin' or pasturing someone who 'loves this present world'… I'd go with the one who committed the sin, and I'll give the reason why.

When you deal with someone who 'loves the world' *"the love of the Father is not in him."* And believe me, that is very hard to work with. How do you 'get a handle' on someone who has no love of God in them? I have tried it for years and from every angle imaginable, *it just doesn't work.* The reason this type of person is almost impossible to work with is found in 1 John 2:15;

"Love not the world, neither the things that are in the world. If any man love the world, the love of the Father is not in him."

On the other hand, I have dealt with people who have fallen into sin, yea even into 'gross immorality' and been able to see them restored and go on and make strong saints for Jesus Christ. They messed up—*but they did not want the world!* They could make it, because—in spite of their sin—they still had the advocate!

"My little children, these things write I unto you, that ye sin not. And if any man sin, we have an advocate with the Father, Jesus Christ the righteous: And he is the propitiation for our sins: and not for ours only, but also for the sins of the whole world." (1 John 2:1-2)

God, give us people who, in spite of their humanity, in spite of their weaknesses, their faults and foibles…*do not love this world*—but do love their Lord and Savior and *advocate*… Jesus Christ.

The Sad History of Holiness Movements

It has been well said that all Holiness movements that have lost their separation lost it over their pleasures and entertainments; be they the Wesleyans, Methodists, Nazarenes, Pentecostal Holiness, Church of God, Assemblies of God or many Oneness movements. Though they all at one time stood for Holiness unto God and separation from the world, it is sadly no longer the case. What we consistently entertain ourselves with will eventually predicate what we are. Small wonder God admonishes us to "**Delight thyself also in the LORD**; and he shall give thee the desires of thine heart." (Ps 37:4)

"Thou wilt keep him in perfect peace, **whose mind is stayed on thee**..." (Isaiah 26:3)

God grant that the Oneness Apostolic Movement of the closing days of this dispensation rise up with a clear, strong, resonant voice of not only evangelism but of righteousness and true holiness. We truly are the people upon whom the ends of the world have come. Let us arise as the three Hebrew children and be not careful to answer in this matter! Genuine—glory revealing—soul saving revival, belongs to the people that not only love souls but the righteous demands of their God as well. History as well as a cursory glance at what is happening in our generation shows this to be so. Let us do as Caleb of old directed; *"Arise, let us go up and take the country!"*